Long Distance Triathlon Memoir

How I Became a Man of Iron with 11 Months Training

Jason Pegler

chipmunkapublishing
the mental health publisher

Jason Pegler

Published by
Chipmunkapublishing
United Kingdom

http://www.chipmunkapublishing.com

ISBN   978-1-78382-063-4

Chipmunkapublishing gratefully acknowledge the support of Arts Council England.

Introduction

This book describes my journey from complete novice to Ironman finisher in 11 months. This is something I am quite proud of, considering I had no swimming, cycling or running background whatsoever.

I've written this book for several reasons. One reason is because I love writing. Another reason is because I want to inspire anyone who is daydreaming about doing an Ironman one day to go for it and live the dream. It really is worth it, and just doing the training is a great lifestyle. Other benefits are that by reliving the experiences, I am working on my craft and will become a better athlete. I am also passionate about setting up some kind of unique and cutting edge Ironman business that offers real value to its clients, as I love the sport and immersing myself in my journey so far is a great way to produce light bulb moments.

Training for and completing my first Ironman made me a better person, a better partner, a better father, a better business owner and improved my health. This is because it made me think bigger and raised my self-esteem.

My promise to you, the inspiring reader, is to give you my all, be honest, not take myself too seriously, and when I do take myself a bit seriously, please remember that I am just sharing my story with you, and everything I have done well and things I could have done better next time along the way.

You may be a multiple Ironman, a professional Ironman athlete (in my dreams, hey?), a coach or a triathlete; you may have a swimming, cycling or running background and be considering taking up the sport, or just have an insane desire to complete the ultimate one-day endurance sporting event that was designed to test the human potential to its limit.

Believe me, it's not easy, but when you cross that finish line there is no feeling quite like it. The more I recall that feeling, the better it actually feels and the more I enjoy it, although I must admit, the first day after completing the Ironman, I had doubts as to whether I would do one again; but the day after that I knew I wanted to do one the following year, and go faster and get a better position in my second Ironman.

Jason Pegler

Why and how did I end up training an Ironman? Am I crazy?

When I was nine years old, I loved sport and was captivated by watching the Ironman World Championships in Hawaii. I swore to myself that, one day, I would do that race and win it. That was in 1984. For the next twenty-eight years I continued to love participating and watching sport, although I do not recall thinking about the phrase 'Ironman' ever again, apart from about the superhero played by Robert Downey Junior in the film.

In July 2012, I was to rekindle my passion for Ironman racing. I walked into my local cycling shop in Crystal Palace with my father and two children, Oscar and Anna. Oscar was four and Anna was nearly two at the time. Whilst following my beloved children around, making sure they had fun learning about cycling and did not break anything, I was asked if I wanted to take part in a free cycling fitness test that was normally £250.The owner of the shop was looking for someone to do the test later that week, as Cycling Weekly were coming round to feature the cycling shop.

The shop was Cycling Cadence Centre in Crystal Palace. It is a state of the art cycling centre (sounds like I am promoting them, hey … damn, forgot to tell them … could have made a few quid there … never mind … next time … lol), with several turbo machines hooked up to giant televisions, so you can ride the famous mountain stages of the Tour De France on stationary bikes. It's also a café, where you can read the cycling or triathlon magazines, mix with other cyclists and stop off for coffee and cake after you have been for a ride.

Still a sporting nut at heart, I immediately said yes, and looked forward to seeing how I would do in the fitness test. I'd been keeping in shape by boxing three times a week at Duke McKenzie's boxing gym in Crystal Palace. Duke is a top bloke, by the way. He always has time for everyone, and at the time of writing, this is the only British boxer to be World Champion in three different weight categories. That really is an amazing achievement. Sorry about that, I just like commenting and getting to know people I admire….

Buzzing about doing the test, I returned a few weeks later. I'd not really ridden a bike since my school days. I had owned one for about a year, from the age of 26 to 27, but hardly ever used it, and sold it for £60 to a second hand cycling shop, losing the money on the way home as it fell out of my pocket, because there were holes in them ... sounds like something only Homer Simpson would do, but I can assure you, I did it....

Anyway, as I was saying, from the age of 11 to 18, I used to ride to and from school most days, often with a giant rucksack full of books on my bike. Most of the time I would ride no handed, as kids do. No wonder I fell off so often.... Over the years that is, not every day, lol. The distance according to Google maps ... ah, technology ... is 3.8 miles each way. That's not exactly Ironman distance, I hear you say, but it must have given me some control on the bike ... I would walk around at school after I got off my bike and play football or rugby at lunch time, so that's not really a brick session, but it would have to do for then....

Oh yeah ... anyway, back to the cycling test. Some guy with a PhD in something sporty was giving me all this information about the test and CO_2 max and all this kind of thing. I was listening attentively, although a lot of it was going in one ear and out the other. I was wearing trainers (no toe clips or anything), and had not ridden a bike regularly for ten years.

As I was preparing to do the test, which was going to get progressively harder every minute, there was a guy next to me who looked super fit.... He was sweating profusely, but talking a lot, and had a big smile on his face. The guy who was helping me get set up for the test adjusted the saddle on the bike so it was more comfortable, and said the most influential words that I was to hear for the next twelve months and who knows how long beyond that:

"Meet Nick, the Ironman."

Immediately I had a Eureka moment ... an epiphany ... seriously ... it hit the core of my being.... It was like a thunderbolt came out of me. The Ironman ... ahhhaaa ... (imagine hearing the Superman theme and seeing Superman flying around to rescue people from a falling skyscraper). It's time ... I remember watching the Ironman on television and knowing somehow I would do it one day....

So, I immediately started chatting to Nick. It turned out that Nick was no ordinary Ironman, even if there is such a thing - which, to be fair, there isn't. Nick was really good at it.

Nick Kinsey used to be the Ironman British record holder. He had done over twenty-five Ironman races in under ten hours by the time I met him, and at the age of fifty-three, was still doing them in nine and a half hours. He has a best time of 8hrs 52 minutes, and was

18th overall in the inaugural Ironman European Championships in Frankfurt in 2000. He is a really good triathlete and has represented Britain in his age group at the Olympic distance, as well as veteran Cyclo Cross Champion. He's run London Marathon 22 times (every time under 3hours) with a best time of 2hrs 25 minutes. He has competed in the Ironman World Championships 3 times coming in the top 5 in his age group, with a best position of 98th overall in The Kona World Championships. Check out his website at www.mallorcaman.co.uk

What a stroke of luck. Nick and I were talking for hours. We immediately got on well, and I was hooked…. During this conversation, I asked him the distance. How long is the Ironman?

It's a 2.4 mile swim, followed by a 112 mile bike ride and then a full marathon 26.2 mile run. I immediately thought, *I can do it… God knows how but I know I can do it.* I also immediately knew that I needed to stay in touch with this guy to make it happen. I was pretty inspired at the time anyway. Both business and family life was going well, and I was looking for a new challenge. I own a publishing business, and had been pretty heavily into personal development, self-hypnosis and neuro linguistic programming for the last decade, so knew that if I was going to make this dream a reality, I had to stay in touch with Nick and learn from him. My thoughts were that in order to achieve anything in a particular area, you need to model the best people in that area and befriend them, spend time with them and mirror, copy, learn from and adapt their techniques to fit your own personal goals.

So we swapped numbers and agreed to meet up for a swim, bike ride and run. I knew my swimming was really weak; although I had swum a mile when I was 9 years old, my technique was terrible. Also, I had probably never done a bike ride more than 12 miles, and that was when I was about 11 years old and would go cycling with my friends every now and then on a Sunday morning. So only another 1.4 miles to swim, another 100 miles to go and a marathon after that.

When I was 11, I had a Raleigh racer that my dad bought me, which had cost £150, and of which I was very proud at the time. The longest run I had ever done was a 5km race in an inter schools cross-country race. I'd come 15th out of 80 runners, which is a lot better than it sounds as the first pack of runners went the wrong way. There must have been about 25 of them, as the best runner from our school came 42nd that day. My other athletic results were coming 9th out of 32 people in my class when told to run around our massive school field during a games lesson, and coming 4th in the 400 metres in the school's sports day. Not exactly Chris McCormack, Craig Alexander or Pete Jacobs territory, but nevertheless, look at the plus side; I could run, was healthy and if anything was undercooked, as opposed to being over-trained.

I knew I had naturally good strength and endurance. There were many times when I had played football for several hours. I used to play rugby 2-3 times a week (then football every lunch time). I played for Gloucester Schools Under 16 at Rugby and got to the last trial for Gloucestershire, but was gutted not to make the team. Up until the calamity at the Rugby trials, I thought I was going to play for England schools and Gloucester first team. That was the dream, and I'd had that dream before rugby had gone professional, which shows how much I loved the game at the time. I always assumed I would play for the Gloucester First Team, but then I turned into a bit of a raver and went off to University.

I'd also been a chess prodigy when I was younger, winning many chess tournaments from the age of nine until I stopped playing at the age of eighteen. My biggest achievements were being ranked fourth in the South and South West of England and winning the Gloucestershire Under 15 Championships. Although, I'd got most satisfaction from coming first out of 243 children when winning the Gloucester Under 11 Championships at the tender age of nine.

My first thoughts were that chess is irrelevant to Ironman training, but then the mental warfare in chess is quite animalistic and similar to what you need in order to keep going through the pain of Ironman in training and race days in triathlon. Although, admittedly, moving some chess pieces around and pressing the clock is less physically demanding for sure....

I figured at the time of meeting Nick that I could probably have completed an Olympic distance triathlon - that's a 1500 metre swim, 40km bike and a 10km run – although, I may not have got through the swim feeling good and would definitely have ended up walking on the run if I hadn't DNF by falling off the bike.

However, I am pretty competitive so I'm pretty sure I could have run some of it. An Ironman, though, would take some real dedication and a big visualization and futuristic thinking. I would get to test my focus, willpower and sheer tenacity. Let's face it; an Ironman is a really long way. Even when I explain the distance to people now, they look at me with a look of utter disbelief.

My first swim, bike and run; I mean, drown, pedal and shuffle

In writing this book, I want to inspire anyone who is thinking of doing an Ironman to do one. I figure the best way to do this is to let you know the exact training I did, what I did well and what I could do better next time. I'll also write about how I kept my belief and the motivation to continue training going and how I overcame any niggles. I've kept daily notes on my note section on my iPhone since I started, so I am going to regurgitate them throughout the text. I'll also try and keep it light hearted, as I know how the daily grind can make it feel impossible. I spent so much time visualising Ironman racing and watching Ironman races on YouTube and the Ironman TV show repeatedly, that I am a real Ironman geek fan. I've also spoken and met quite a few of the pros (more of that later), as once you do one Ironman, you either give up or you want to go even quicker next time. So relax and strap yourself in to hear those amazing words for yourself....

You are an Ironman and remember that there is one day ... an amazing day ... when you push yourself to the ultimate limits of human endurance.... The Ironman 220km or 140.6 miles is the ultimate physical and psychological test. It's what it makes of you, this momentous day, that really counts.... How far can you push yourself? How far can you push your body? To the extreme.... Which can push itself further, your mind or your body? Or will one of them pack in? Something is going to go wrong in the race but, like life, it's how you react to it that determines where you end up.... Never give up.... Never give up.... And reach the unknown strengths that you never knew you had.... So you can wear that Ironman medal round your neck ... and hear those infamous words ... "you are an Ironman" ... and then have a well-deserved break afterwards, although you might want to queue up for a couple of hours the next day in the blazing sun and enter the same race you just completed for the following year before it sells out again....

I just dug out my training notes from my iPhone, which I have been typing on daily for the last thirteen months.... Later on in this book, I will break down every week of training throughout the year that I can find and tell you what I did well, where I went wrong and how I stayed motivated. First I'll tell you how Nick Kinsey, my coach, and I decided to map out the year.

Nick suggested training for a few weeks and then seeing if I really wanted to do it. Then the plan was to buy a decent bike and enter a race. He also suggested that we go for a swim, bike and run.

We met up at the start of July in the John Lloyd Fitness Centre in Beckenham, where Nick arranged a free day pass for me. First we got in the pool. Nick told me to swim two lengths. It was only a twenty-five metre pool. I swam the first twenty-five metres front crawl, moving my head around so much, quite frankly embarrassed, and then breast-stroked back. During the next forty five minutes or so, Nick proceeded to tell me a million things I did not know about swimming as I followed him in the lane, until he shot off as if he was in a speedboat. It made me think that I must have looked like I was drowning. I realised that my swimming was absolutely rubbish. Thing is, I was so interested in what Nick was saying, and so determined, that it did not really upset my confidence yet. Nick also said that I had a lot of power in my breaststroke kick, which gave me a lot of confidence and led me mistakenly to daydream about breast-stroking the whole 2.4 miles.

Then we got changed. I noticed how slim and toned Nick was and realised I had a much bigger belly than I thought. A lot of unused muscle, I liked to call it. I was 85 kilos, although I am 6ft 3 ½ - that's 190.5 cm if you are from the US or Spain, by the way. I was not really overweight; however, a year later, I was the same weight but had a completely different body shape, with a lot more muscle.

Ah, yes ... sorry about the vanity.... It's a characteristic of mine from time to time.... Still got a lot of work to do to build my muscles ... did you know you peak as an Ironman in your 10th year apparently, if you keep doing the right training? There's hope for all of us to get that Kona slot, and who knows ... win one's age group or even get on the podium.... Some of us can dream of being World Champion. The event is so difficult, and there are only a few people that have ever won it, largely thanks to the all-time greats Dave Scott, Mark Allen, Paula Newby Fraser and Natascha Badman, who have won it twenty-six times between them.

Ah, to dream ... that's right, just sit back and relax ... and dare to dream ... to design the life and outcome you really want.... Close your eyes... step out of yourself ... your eyes ... go back to when you were a little child, and think of a time when you knew you could achieve anything you wanted to in life ... that's right... see what you saw ... hear what you heard ... and feel what you felt.... Now, go into your future and imagine achieving something that you've always wanted to do ... that's right, be there ... now ... see how great it is to have achieved something you always wanted to ... make the picture bigger and bigger ... brighter and brighter.... Congratulate yourself ... really take in all the senses ... what do you look like in the picture of your newfound success? What can you hear? Turn up the feeling … make the picture bigger and brighter.... That's right … now come back to the present moment … and step back into yourself, in time … and open your eyes.... Feel good? I hope so.... ☺

So there's hope for most of us … you and me.... If you've peaked already, then I'm sure you still get a buzz out of the Ironman addiction … I know I do. Lol....

Anyway, we got on these bikes in the gym. They were like BMX bikes attached to a computer, and you play a game. Nick and I raced against virtual opponents, and cycled for about twenty minutes. I thought I was doing really well, especially as Nick took a couple more minutes setting up his program, so I felt like I was ahead. However, he finished way before and I think he was on a harder level as well. Also, he didn't look tired either, so I guess that says it all. Then I thought we had finished, but in the changing room he said:

"Right, let's go for a run."

I said that I was feeling a bit tired, but then he said something like:

"It will only be a short run at a steady pace … how do you know if you want to do an Ironman, unless you try all three in a row?"

So we went outside into the car park. It was absolutely boiling and I was already exhausted. Probably more psychologically than physically tired, but aching in places a little bit.

Nick goes off at a quick pace … my first requests were to keep asking if we could slow down a bit … by the time we'd run for about ten minutes, I'd realised we had not turned back, so mentally stopped resisting and started to enjoy it.... Nick kept telling me how to run, saying things like:

"Run light … on your toes a bit ... head up … pump your arms back and forward and rotate your legs up and down like a bike … head straight … look ahead...."

Every three or four minutes, he would say:

"Right, let's pick up the pace for 100 metres; you cannot stay locked in at the same pace...."

I was so relieved when we were coming back round the block, as I knew the run was nearly over ... but I felt quite good ... out of breath a bit ... but it was manageable, and I knew it was nearly over. We probably only ran about three miles, if that.

A few minutes later, we were having a coffee and a chat ... I felt like it was possible. I got home, excited and ready to make my move.... Kona, here I come, lol.... Yeah, right....

Swim, Bike, Run training for the first time … training volume, buying the kit and entering my first Ironman….

So during July 2012, I started my first month of Ironman training. Nick had me on around 5-8 hours a week to see if I liked it, which would increase over later months as the Ironman loomed, if I was up for it:

Weekly hours for completing my first Ironman safely:

August: 6-8
September: 5-8
October: 5-8
November: 6.5-8
December: 6-8
January: 7-9
Feb: 8-10
March: 10-14 (13,10,12,8)
April: 11-15 (15,10,12,14)
May: 8-12 (9,11,13,8)
June: (10,12,7,5)

(The numbers in brackets indicate number of hours anticipated per week during that month, although things rarely go according exactly to plan).

One thing I learnt was to congratulate myself whenever I did a session, and to forgive myself if I missed one or did not go the full amount of time. Most Ironman training books recommend training by time as opposed to distance, as it's then easier to fit into your life timetable….

Also, one of the good tips I read from Chris McCormack's autobiography is to cut a training session 20% short if it's not going to plan, and have time to assess it and refuel, instead of exhausting yourself or injuring yourself and not taking in your recovery food.

It is much better to be slightly undercooked than overcooked. Over-training leads to exhaustion and injury…. However, you need consistent training and the right kind of training to be ready for race day. Having Nick there throughout gave me real focus and confidence.

Be honest with yourself though, and avoid using this as an excuse to bottle it or not do your best.

The training for July 2012, my first ever month of Ironman training, would be broken down as follows.

3x 30-45min runs, 1 easy, 1 medium and 1 fast, and 2x 1hr swims, all front crawl, with pull buoy and some core work in the gym.

The bike rides would start mid-August, as I needed to buy a bike first, so I continued to do some core work in the gym, and said goodbye to my boxing career with Duke McKenzie for the time being ... lol. The cycle practice would start off as two 1x 1.5-2hr bike rides, and then ramp up in volume along with the swimming and running during 2013, before a taper with Ironman Klagenfurt loomed nicely in June 2013.

Buying the kit – how much?

So I decided to get some kit, sharpish … and made some contingency plans for spending over the eleven months until my first Ironman race.

Spend from July 2012 - £3,150
£1,600 bike. I bought a Felt A5, on Nick's advice. It was the previous year's model and was discounted by around £700. It's a racing bike … later on we would be adding some tri bars, but first I had to get used to riding it.

£500 Bike Gear
Helmet, £60. Shades, £30. Gloves, £30. Lycra shorts and tops, mostly dhb stuff, £200. Spare inner tubes, £20. Mini pump, £15; decent pump, £50. Water bottles and cages, £25; £50 energy bars and gels. Assos Chamois Cream, £10 x 2, to put on your bum and surrounding areas so you do not get sore. Very important!

£220 Running Gear
One pair of Asics trainers, £70. Tops, shorts and caps, £150.

£150 Coach
Five sessions at £30 per hour.

Ironman Entry and Accommodation Deposit - £700

Once I factored in buying more kit, including wetsuit, winter running gear, Garmin 910 (that's £350; you can get a decent Garmin for £100 with bike and run heart rates and distance, but you won't be able to record the swim), bike jacket, more trainers, etc., over the rest of the year, as well as flights, accommodation, nutrition and paying for additional coaching (that's another £2,500 over the year), the total spend for my first year in Ironman turned out to be about £6,000. There's probably another £1,000 that I forgot to mention, to be honest, but I went a bit over the top.

Realistically, someone could do this for a lot less, probably for around £3,000 for a full twelve months, as I bought a lot of kit, did my first Ironman abroad so had to pay flights and accommodation and paid extra by entering my Ironman race through Nirvana Europe, as it was initially sold out. It is worth spending £1,000 on a decent bike and getting a decent wetsuit for at least £200, and I would highly recommend a coach, which you could get for £30 a session. You can coach yourself through Jo Friel's infamous

Triathlon Training Bible, and it is a must read, but learning technique and how to approach training and racing from someone who has actually done some Ironmans with a decent time is going to give you more confidence and make the whole thing seem more real and achievable.

I never bought an aero helmet or any aero wheels, which are expensive. You are looking at £1,500 for a couple of Zipp wheels, but I recommend leaving that for your first Ironman, as although they will make you go quicker on the flat especially, the most important thing is for you to learn to handle the bike safely, and aero wheels mean a lighter bike in the wind.... I do not have my aero wheels and helmet yet, but I plan on getting them.... Kona, here we come, lol....

Enter Your Ironman

The most decisive moment for me, and I believe for anyone wanting to complete an Ironman, was to commit to entering an Ironman by paying for it a long time in advance.

For weeks, I had been discussing with Nick which was the best Ironman race to enter. Nick suggested Frankfurt or Klagenfurt as the two best races in Europe. Nick entered Frankfurt and, as I procrastinated, it very quickly sold out, as did Klagenfurt. He advised Klagenfurt, as it was a fast course with a swim in a lake and a fast bike course, so I picked that. I did this by entering through an Ironman travel agent called Nirvana Europe, which buys Ironman tickets. As long as you book your accommodation with them, you can purchase your ticket with them, albeit at around £150 more than it would be if you bought it on ironman.com before they sold out.

The moment I entered Klagenfurt, it was like the whole thing became 100 times more real. I became totally focused and probably obsessed with completing the race, which was not until June 2013, some eleven months away. The fact that I did this in my first few weeks of training was a massive psychological boost that gave me huge motivation and momentum to complete my sessions. I already saw myself as an Ironman and just needed to do everything I could to make it happen come crunch time.

I started to watch YouTube videos of all the great Ironman World Championship races at home. Thank God for YouTube. Top of my list was the infamous 1989 "Iron war" between Dave Scott and Mark Allen. Dave Scott was the six-time champion, and was practically unbeatable in the humidity of Kona, until Mark Allen finally managed to become victorious and come first after several years of heartache. The two had been head to head, wheel to wheel and elbow to elbow the entire race, and obliterated the rest of the field. With only a couple of miles to go, Dave grabbed for a drink at the last drinks station, and Mark said that something in his mind went go and it was like he was "shot out of a cannon".

That's a bit like I felt the moment I entered Klagenfurt, although I was clumsier and less cannon-like than Mark. During training, I actually ran into a lamppost and rode into a ditch, but managed to carry on both times.

Seriously though, a golden nugget of advice for you is to enter the race way in advance. I would recommend an official Ironman race if you can afford it (see ironman.com), as that is how triathlon and Ironman started. They are also brilliantly organised; people come from all over the world, and it gets you close to the source of energy you need to complete an Ironman (only joking, although, for me, I think there really was something in that ... anyway, back to the story, or, dare I say, guide....)

By entering the race well in advance, I was fully committed. I knew what lay ahead ... I was totally excited and absolutely terrified. That was my yin and yang. I then set about telling everyone I saw about it. That was a big driving factor in me taking the plunge to meet up with Nick, enter the race and continue the training, which is a huge commitment in anyone's life. By telling everyone about it, you become accountable, as next time you see people they will always ask you how the training's going, guaranteed ... this unconsciously and consciously drives you to carry out your training. It's also a nice thing to do, as you would be amazed how many people it encourages to exercise more regularly. I told hundreds of people within the first couple of months of entering, and found myself as an unpaid fitness mentor, instructor and consultant, all of a sudden. That was a lot of pro bono work, I am telling you.... The more accountable you are to other people, the more likely you are to complete your goal.... That goes with anything in life, and it goes big time with something as hard-core as doing an Ironman....

How do I fit the training in?

Everyone's lives are busy. It's all a matter of perception really. I am lucky to have my own businesses, so my working time is flexible, although my two children were four and two years old when I started training for Klagenfurt (which is in Austria, and is a beautiful place to do your first Ironman by the way, although it can get mega-hot there, as you will see later on).

I knew what my training was at least a few weeks in advance most of the time. I think that it is really helpful to know your training at least a few weeks in advance, preferably a month in advance if possible. This way, you can manage your life with Ironman included, and everyone and everything else in some kind of equilibrium as well.

What I found was that if I could get my session or one of my two sessions in earlier, then mostly it was and still is:

1) Easier to do, as you have more energy then
2) You feel better for the day, as you have the endorphins from exercising
3) You feel more confident an athlete, as you have hit your target early on
4) You can then look forward to your next session, as you did the last one
5) You also feel good about yourself the whole day, as you have completed the session.

I understand that everyone has different commitments, so just fit your sessions in whenever you can. Tell yourself you are going to do them beforehand, see yourself doing it and feel how good you are going to feel when you start, whilst you are doing it and after you have done it. Do whatever it takes to complete your sessions. If you end up missing one, forgive yourself and get on with nailing the next session.

Completing an Ironman is a very tough task for even the most committed person. The more consistent you are in your training, the more chance you have of doing yourself justice and completing the event come race day.

Your biggest ally come race day is the preparation, preparation and preparation beforehand. This means training six days a week for the six months before, at least, and probably for a longer duration if you are a novice and have no swimming, cycling or running back ground, especially.

The books I've read suggest you should have a background in at least one of the sports, and should then build up your training over a two year period. I managed to do it in ten months, because I was committed enough to do my training and learn everything I could about the sport over that period of time. Without the consistent training, the wheels would have fallen off, no matter how determined I was. It's not known as the hardest one-day endurance event in the world for nothing.

Training for and completing an Ironman is of course an extremely demanding psychological and physical challenge. I think it's also important to know that it is also only really for people who have the time and money to commit to it.

Hypnotise yourself

The moment I decided I was going to complete an Ironman, I immediately hypnotised myself into believing that I would do it. Then I visualised myself actually doing it, felt what it would feel like and heard myself saying that I'd done it.

Get into NLP - Neuro Linguistic Programming

One of my main belief strategies, which assisted me in completing an Ironman with so little background in triathlon and swimming, cycling or running, is that I knew I could use my skills I had developed in NLP to make it happen. I studied successful Ironman athletes from the moment I became interested in competing. NLP is all about modelling excellence, and reprogramming your brain to get more done, be happier and achieve more in life. If you want to benefit from it, I recommend you study the guy who invented it, Richard Bandler, and nobody else. Without wanting to sound like a bit of a weirdo, I believe that in 100 years' time, they will talk about Einstein, Newton and Bandler as the three most influential people during that period in history.

I studied my coach, Nick: how he did each of the three disciplines; how he approached racing; what he ate; how he approached training. I watched endless hours of Ironman World Championship videos and many other Ironman related videos on YouTube, including when doing just about every winter turbo session in my garage. Although I do have to admit, a few times I ended up watching some Personal Development Seminars on YouTube instead – a bit of Jim Rohn, or Anthony Robbins - to pump me up even more and keep me focused on completing the training and not giving up.

I read several books on how to complete an Ironman, and the autobiographies of Ironman World Champions like Chris McCormack and Chrissie Wellington.

Jason Pegler

Setting Bigger Goals

I would be lying if I said that there were some days when I did not feel like training. I liked the idea of Ironman as a lifestyle, so I constantly imagined competing in Ironman races until I was at least fifty years of age. I was thirty-seven when I started training in August 2012. This made one Ironman seem a lot more achievable. I also imagined going up to Ultramarathons, and watched tough races like the Badwater Ultramarathon on YouTube. It's a 153mile running race through Death Valley.

I found that my confidence stumbled a little bit from time to time around December/January 2013 with the sheer enormity of the distance of the race playing on my mind. In order to give myself a new lease of life, I decided to read some more inspirational autobiographies. I read a book by Jason Lester entitled 'Running On Faith'. Now, this guy could do five Ironman races in five days and double Ironman's. Pretty cool, I hear you say…. But he did them without being able to use his right arm properly. His arm was paralysed when he was younger in an accident. His determination and work ethic is relentless. One day he was doing a double Ironman and was being stung by hundreds of jellyfish. He was taken into a boat and treated for the stings, and his crew thought he was finished, but he got back out there and completed the race. Now if this guy could do that with an arm missing, I could complete Klagenfurt and any niggling pains during my training. His name is also Jason; that meant I was halfway there.

I had two massive goals on my phone and I would add notes to my Ironman training on my iPhone every day. The two insane goals were:

1)   Win Kona Ironman World Championships in November 2022 – guess that made completing Klagenfurt in 2013 seem easier, and I dare to dream big.

2)   December 2023, win Sports Personality of the Year – well, if I were World Champion, and considering that the popularity of Ironman is increasing year on year, it would be great to see Ironman athletes benefitting from the publicity that professionals from other sports benefit from.

These massive, *ridiculous* goals gave me momentum. Richard Bandler (the founder of Neuro Linguistic Programming), Donald Trump (the entrepreneur and property tycoon), Brian Tracy (one of the leaders in personal development and goal setting); they all say to think big and set big goals. If I was aiming to be World Champion by 2022, then I would definitely complete Ironman Klagenfurt in June 2013.

Also, in order to win Sports Personality of the Year, I'd have to be really good at marketing myself and probably have to write an International Best Selling book, or several, on Ironman, to help other people enjoy the sport that I had just fallen in love with. The writing the book part seemed quite feasible, as I wrote a book in 2002 called 'A Can of Madness', which did rather well and enabled me to launch the world's main mental health publishing company, Chipmunkapublishing.

In 2022 I would be forty-eight years old, which would be ten years older than Craig 'Crowie' Alexander was when he won The Ironman World Championships in 2011. I'd have to re-define the laws of the anatomy and motivation, and look for other inspirational older athletes. One who springs to mind is the world plank record holder George Hood, who, in April 2013, increased his own world record to three hours, at the age of fifty-five.... Yes, that's right. That's the same plank position that makes most people start shaking after thirty seconds, and have to stop after a minute or one and half minutes.

Then there is the famous Australian farmer, whose name I forget, whose story is told on the personal development circuit seminar by Anthony Robbins and Jack Canfield. His story goes to show how much you can achieve if your mind is unlimited in belief, drive, ambition, determination and confidence. Let me explain. He entered an Ultramarathon race that was approximately six days long. He was one of the oldest competitors. Everyone starts off, running quickly in his or her trendy gear, and this guy is in his farmer's clothes bringing up the rear.... Everyone else goes to sleep in his or her tents. This guy carries on going, running through the night, every night, as nobody else tells him otherwise. He is one of the oldest competitors in the race, and ends up winning and breaking the course record. How did he achieve this? Well he was pretty fit, being a farmer, but the main thing was that his mind-set was so much better than everyone else. He had unlimited drive, demonstrated by his continued running throughout the night. He saw what was possible.

There is a crucial difference in the psychology of winning between the champions and the nearly-champions. What makes people like Dave Scott, Mark Allen, Paula Newby Fraser, Scott Tinley, Peter

Reid, Chris McCormack, Chrissie Wellington, Miranda Carefrae and Craig Alexander multiple champions? They may or may not have greater athletic ability than the other top professionals. One thing they have for certain is a greater belief. The margins between 1st and 2nd or 1st and 10th in the Ironman World Championships are very small, but so significant at the highest level.

The same goes with the very top entrepreneurs, musicians, chefs, etcetera; whatever it is, there is a slightly different mind-set, and that's the difference between being a Stephen Hendry or a Jimmy White. The two aforementioned snooker players have a different record, Hendry with seven World Championship final appearances and seven victories, and White with six runner-up spots and no victories. Once White was leading Hendry 14-10, but then went on to lose 18-14. Snooker fans often say that White was more talented but Hendry's superior mind-set, belief, focus or need to win was so superior that he ended up being the best of all time. This je ne sais quoi is possibly what makes the difference between first and second, more often than not.

Jason Pegler

Back To The Training

So, the training for July, my first ever Ironman training, was 3 x 30-45 min runs, 1 easy, 1 medium and 1 fast, 2 x 1 hour swims, all front crawl with pull buoy.

The bike rides were to start in mid-August, as I needed to buy a bike first.... ☺

For the running, I chose the same route most of the time to start with. At the time of training, I lived in Crystal Palace, London. It's very hilly around Crystal Palace. I chose to do my runs either in a field, if my legs were aching, which included five minutes running on concrete there and back, but most of the time was able to run through the main shops in Crystal Palace and then down towards Dulwich park. Nick was quite insistent on me running on the road, as long as my legs did not ache, and wanted me to avoid treadmills, especially as it is not the same as running on the road. If you run flat on a treadmill, then you do not have to pump your arms forward like you do when running. I've read that you should add a 1% gradient to make it more realistic, although Nick recommended a 3-5% gradient, so I tried to run on the pavement as much as I could, and then trails or grass sometimes and treadmills as a last option.

I immediately purchased a Garmin 110 with heart rate monitor, which I must say motivated me massively. It took the pain out of running, as I could disassociate from the pain, and look at how far I was running and at what pace. Also, the first half of the run was downhill, which was a bit of a confidence booster, as it made me quicker than it seemed. However, the run on the way back is really steep coming up Gipsy Hill.

The first time I wore my new Asics to run in was actually on the treadmill in the gym, as I was quite into core training at the time, from my time boxing with Duke McKenzie. I felt a bit of a pain, and when I took my shoes off, one of my toenails was bleeding. Remarkably, that was the only time I was to have bleeding toenails or aching toes when running over the next year, even on Ironman race day in Klagenfurt. That's not to say that I did not have aches everywhere else, but my toes were OK after that.

With my new bike, I was mostly focused on staying upright. It took me a few weeks until I got a bike, and then the first time I went out on it was around Crystal Palace Park with Nick. The trickiest part was clipping in and out of the pedals and avoiding dogs running around the park. I'd used toe clips at school on my racer, so I was aware that you'd have to get your feet out pretty quickly if necessary.

Nick taught me something so important and useful, but so simple, that I nearly passed out. He taught me to break with both brakes at the same time and gently or just use the front/back break. This was a huge Eureka moment in my cycling career. Why, I hear you ask excitedly?

Please let me explain. From the age of 11-18, I rode my bike every day to and from school, whilst carrying an enormous Karrimor rucksack, usually containing fifteen books and my rugby kit inside it. The ride to school was around four miles each way, with a really steep sharp hill in between. Over the years, I fell off my bike many times. The main reason was because I usually rode no-handed whilst speaking to my friends, but also when losing control I would always touch the break on my left or slam both brakes on. Nick told me to use the other break or slightly pepper them. It gave me better control immediately.

I felt like I could be the next Lance Armstrong, but that was before we discovered that he was a cheat, so Bradley Wiggins or Chris Froome will definitely do … or even Chris Lieto or Sebastian Kienle will more than do.

Nick took me out for a ride in the North Downs or South Downs - I always get them confused - and took me up Whites Hill. The hill is legendary with cyclists. Nick told me that if I could not make it up to just walk up and he would wait for me at the top. Always up for a challenge, I went for it, and as Nick slowly disappeared into the distance, I pedalled really quickly in the easiest gear, probably going slower than it would take to walk in the end, but made it to the top keeping my feet in the pedals. Nick was very impressed, saying that most people he took up there first time around could not make it and that I had done really well.

I went out a couple of times with Nick on the bike in the early days. Once he took a sharp left on a really sharp downhill slope. It must have been about 20-25% and was covered in stones and rocks. I nearly fell off. Had I fallen, it would have been a hospital job or a graze worse than Chrissie Wellingtons was just two weeks before she won her third or fourth Ironman world title.

It was clear he had much better control of me on the bike, and that going downhill was the most dangerous from my point of view. Another time, he was going so fast downhill, that I failed to avoid some glass when trying to keep up and ended up with a puncture. Thankfully, Nick was there to help me fix it.

Over the course of the year I was to get more confident on the bike, and even though I went out with a friend a few times called Warren, who can do a 25 mile time trial in under an hour, so he is pretty handy, I felt safer and still do feel safer riding on my own. I also love the challenge of riding on my own and not drafting, and the mental challenge of seeing how fast I can go against myself. With the Garmin as my companion, I stick to similar routes in case I get lost, but they are tough rides and I push myself hard.

The early swim sessions were really enjoyable. I was focussing on technique, and let's face it; the pull buoy makes it a lot easier. It definitely helped me to turn my shoulders and keep my head still, which is essential if you are going to save energy for an Ironman and not look like a complete muppet when swimming.

I found I could swim for sixty minutes straight away, although I would end up stopping every 50 metres for a couple of seconds to be honest, as I had no flip turn, and would have needed to take a longer breath even if I could.

To take the boredom away from the swimming and give me confidence, I would often visualise Brian Tracy sayings and mantras and repeat them in my head. Like: "I can do it" .... "I like myself" ... and make up my own ... "I am an Ironman...." These incantations were to be useful throughout my training. By visualising that I was already an Ironman, it kind of made it psychologically easier.... There were moments when training for Ironman got really tough, so I would watch YouTube videos on the Badwater 135 mile Ultramarathon, or read about Dean Karnazes, the Ultramarathon Man.... This made the tough days easier, and changed my mind-set to more of a belief and I-can-do-it attitude. It meant I was raising my standards, and therefore raising my game and ability to finish the Ironman when the real test arrived on race day.

Nick also told me to get hold of the Total Immersion swimming videos by the American Terry Laughlin and do the drills.... Terry was a good swimmer when he was younger, but not the greatest. He prided himself on his work ethic. He became a swim coach, and noticed differences between the way some swimmers seem to swim effortlessly and others seem to have to work harder. The Total Immersion DVDs definitely did help my swimming and made me think about being streamlined and being relaxed in the water, although I did not do the drills that required you to stand up in the water, as the pool in Crystal Palace has no shallow end. So I did not get as much out of them as I could have. It was just too much of an effort to go to different swimming pools throughout the week to do different workouts. Nick was setting me different drills all the time, anyway, and explaining why I was doing them, whether it was swimming with my fists or fingertips brushing the water.

I watched the videos often on the computer, sometimes when on the turbo and occasionally in the evenings. I bought one DVD for freestyle in the pool and one specifically for freestyle in the open water. Total Immersion did make me focus on technique, and gave me a much better mind-set towards swimming as the weeks and months went by.

There were some problems later on with my swimming, mainly my left knee hurting sometimes I went back to using the pull buoy, although come race day it went better than imagined. It is definitely a lot easier in a wetsuit, so the more training you do in the pool, the better. This increases your confidence when it is time to wear the wetsuit, as you are quicker than you think and get less tired. However, swimming in a wetsuit has its own complications, so for my next Ironman I am going to do more practice swimming in the wetsuit.

When I swam the Ironman in Austria, it was only the fourth time I'd ever swum in a wetsuit. The first time was with Nick about six weeks before the race, the second time was a half Ironman, the third time was in the lake in Klagenfurt a couple of days before the race and the fourth time was race day. I had practiced taking it on and off a couple of times at home. In fact, I bought a Blueseventy Helix first time around, but it was so small that I returned it. Nick had told me to get a tight wetsuit, as did Dan Bullock, who Nick had sent me to in February/March to help bring my swimming along, as I was finding it difficult.

Up until then, I did not see my time improve much, and found that I was missing some of the sessions, sometimes only swimming once a week instead of the two we were scheduling. A couple of lessons with Dan did help. He runs Swim For Tri, has been a swimming coach since 1990 and has swum 3.8km in under 45 minutes. He videoed my stroke and I could not believe how bad it looked. I thought I swam a lot more "beautifully" than I actually did.

He told me to point my toes inwards, as they were creating too much drag and sinking my body, and to point my legs together and even brush them together. He also said to kick straighter and give smaller kicks. He gave me several drills to focus on using a really small float, and we increased my swims to 3x 45 minute swims a week. I was also to strengthen my core and ankle flexibility with dry land exercises every day. It worked fairly well. About a month before the Ironman I stopped doing the dry land exercises completely, as I did not want to tire myself out before the big day. I was aware of wanting to be undercooked than overcooked, as I had put so much effort in for such a long time. I was relearning my stroke with my feet, but only went to two lessons, so did not discuss my rotation or arms movements much. As far as I understand Dan's website, he focuses more on that in later lessons, although he did mention it a bit, and some of the drills were meant to improve that as well. It's hard to remember which drill did what exactly to be honest, but it did give me more confidence in my swimming, which was crucial at the time.

The Total Immersion DVDs were good. They teach you how to swim with less effort. This is massively helpful in Ironman, as the more energy you can save during the swim the better. I went from being completely rubbish to quite poor in Ironman terms over the space of the year, but I am still improving all the time. I found I made more significant improvements when I had a lesson with Harry Wiltshire in October 2013.

The swim is the shortest part of the race in time, so if you are not a great swimmer, or even a good one, it shows that you can still complete an Ironman … that's if I did complete it; you'll have to read on to see how well I did … lol…. As I said, I could not do some of the Total Immersion drills, as I trained in Crystal Palace Pool, where it is not possible to stand in the water. Looking back, I would have been better going to another pool to master the earlier drills, but we all learn something along the way.

As far as my notes go, my first week in August 2012 training must have been a continuation of the weeks in July, as I did not write each day down. From the 12th of August, I wrote every week down.

I really think it will help you to see my training each week, and some of the statistics involving distance and heart rate and types of training, if you are yet to do an Ironman and doubting whether you can do it, or wondering how many years it will take you to build up to it. If you plan it into your life and do the correct kind of training, focusing on technique and building your aerobic and anaerobic training at the right time, then it is definitely possible.

Watching the Ironman World Championships on YouTube, the way it's all marketed kind of makes it seem impossible. Indeed, when you say it to the average person in the street, you see people's eyes and they say it's insane, impossible or that they could never do that. Like anything in life, it's a mind-set. Many of the people I described it to asked me to repeat the distance again, with a jaw-dropping look of utter disbelief on their faces.

However, as in life, where you focus on is where you end up, and life is too short not to go for your dreams. As I am writing this, the celebrity chef Gordon Ramsey has just completed Kona for the first time, in 14 hours. In fact, he says in a video on the official Ironman website that he is so hooked on Ironman, he is aiming to set up new restaurants where there are Ironman races that he has not yet done, so he can tick them off his list. Now David Beckham is even talking about doing one, which would be a great profile-raiser for the sport.

Gordon Ramsey describes Ironman as being brilliant because it is the time when he gets time alone to himself, and we all need that. For me and many others, this is part of that magical time when we can take time to focus on our own lives, our own dreams, heal ourselves, know thyself; whatever you want to call it ... be in spiritual balance ... the equilibrium of life ... the power of now ... heightened consciousness ... super consciousness ... total relaxation ... Karma ... meditation ... relieving stress ... or just see what we are really made of on one particular day.

For me, the Ironman journey is one of discovery. It's the hardest thing I can possibly think of, apart from a double Ironman, so it pushes me to do better in every other aspect of my life, be that relationships, love, business, parenting or contribution to the world - whatever it is.

Having given some general insights into what I hope will be really useful for anyone who is doing Ironman for the first time, the rest of the book is going to focus on going through my notes from the beginning of my coaching with Nick, all the notes I took from all the texts and everything I read online, in magazines and in Ironman books etc. This way, I will be sure not to miss anything out that could be useful for you in helping you to achieve your Ironman goal, or just enjoying how someone else achieved his or hers.

Week 6 - Training week 12th of August 2012

Sunday: 30-minute run
Monday: 35-minute bike
Tuesday: 30-minute swim, 20-minute run, 35-minute bike
Wednesday: 45-minute run, 20-minute gym core strength
Thursday: 1hr bike
Friday: Swim 50 minutes. 1,500 metres, no kicking. Using pull buoy.
5k run anaerobic (on treadmill) – 24 minutes, 15 seconds. 20 minutes weights. Stretch.

6hrs 10 minutes this week.

Week 7…. I've bought a bike!! A Felt. Got it reduced from £2,200 to £1,500 as it was end of season model.

Starts Monday August 20th 2012:

Monday: 45-minute run - 4.2 miles
Tuesday: 45-minute run - 4.5 miles
Wednesday: 1hr swim - 46 laps, 2300 metres.
Thursday: 1hr bike (new bike, with Nick)
Friday: 1hr swim - 47 laps, 2350 metres. Using pull buoy to gain better body position for the future. 35-minute run - 5.2km. 1hr 15m core (6hrs 20m)
Saturday - Rest
Sunday – Rest

Tips. When swimming - keep eyes down
Pull recovery, kick, breathing. Elbow above waist and fingers down.

New kit:
- Wiggle - dhb - cycle top - £30-40
- Endura - Polaris - cycle tops - £60
- Bike Helmet - £40-£50 - lighter, better.

Points of interest taken from notes on my iPhone, August 2012:

- Talcum powder for feet when running on race day.

- If injury, ice an affected area 2-3 times a day, 15-20 minutes. Deep tissue massage, foam rollers, art active release techniques. (This means I must have had sore legs, probably knees, from not being used to running and not having a great running style.)

- Get fuel belt for running – makes your transitions quicker and saves vital seconds in races.

- Top of saddle to the middle of the bottom bracket is 76.5cm, 30 inches. Bike saddle - inside leg 80cm, 31.5 inch

Dear reader - you will need to measure these and other areas for when you get your bike fit and if you have to take your bike apart for travelling to an Ironman race.

- Sun cream for race is mega important. Use P20 – It's the best sunblock that lasts 24 hours. It's really expensive, but it's worth it! The sun cream they give you at races will fall off.

- Base, build, peak, taper – this is the order of the training process throughout the year to get race ready.

- Cadence monitor must be 90-95. 75 cadence is too stressful on body, and will come back to haunt you.

- Dioralyte has salts in it and rehydrates the body. Sun tan lotion and mix drinks the morning of the race.... Nick says Dioralyte is essential for him, and also for someone who has finished all but one of the 30 odd Ironman races he has ever raced and finished hundreds, possibly thousands, of other races, most of the Ironmans in 9 hours and some even under 9 hours; that's good enough for me.

Ironman distance:
2.4-mile swim - 3.8km
112-mile bike - 180 km
26.2 mile run - 42km

I am not sure if it seems longer in kilometres or in miles. There's no escaping it. It's the same distance whatever metrics you use, and it's still a really long way. Writing the distance down for me felt like setting a goal, and writing it down both in kilometres and miles busied my mind so I could get on with training. Sounds weird, but it's true.

1km = 1000 metres
1km = 0.62 miles

1mile = 1609 metres

I wrote the conversions between kilometres, metres and miles down to break down different aspects of my training when looking at my training at my Garmin and looking after sessions. It definitely inspired me to keep running when I saw I was reaching 5km, 10km and looking at the times seeing improvements or at the end of a mile. Also, when you feel good you can count off a mile; when it's not going so well you can count the kilometres in your head instead, and it seems like you've run further. As I got more confident with all of my disciplines I'd look at my Garmin watch less, but still probably looked at it too much and still do.

Craig Alexander's Ironman World Champion 2011 split and Kona record:

8hrs 3mins total - swim 51.56mins, bike 4hrs 24mins, run 2hrs 44mins.

These times show what's possible. If Craig Alexander can do this time in Kona, then I can do a better Ironman time than I initially thought. Right? Well, hopefully. Let's see later on....

2.4-mile swim, 3.8km, is 3800 metres - 76 lengths of the 50-metre Crystal Palace pool.

Every time I wrote that down, it seemed like a long way. Although the more often I went swimming, the easier it became. Then Dan Bullock told me later that most people swim 4km in Ironman, as they don't swim straight. Uh oh....

18/8/2012 – 87.5 kilos, 192lbs, 13st 10lbs – surely a bit too heavy. What weight should I go down to? 78 kilos? 171lbs, 12st 2lbs. Maybe that's too light. I got to 85 kilos on race day. From February to June, my weight stayed pretty much the same. I went to see Duke McKenzie in January, and he told me I looked too thin and had lost too much weight. He told me to eat loads of pasta, and I was not going to argue with the Duke. However, as Dave Scott told me in September 2013, a few months after Klagenfurt, it's pretty clear that the best Ironman athletes are pretty lean.

My Ironman target - if under 12 hours, my approximate splits would be:
Swim - 1hr 30min
Bike - 5hr 45min

Run - 4hr 30min
Transitions - 10 minutes
Total here is 11hrs 55 minutes.

That would be cool. Let's get on with the training.

30/7/12

Level 1: 100-120
Level 2: 120-130 (lower)
Level 2 upper: 130-140
Level 3: 140-150
Level 4: 150-160
Level 5: 160-180

This is the typical heart rate zones written down. When testing my heart rate on quick runs, I found I could get mine up to 190-195 if I really pushed. If it got any higher, it was because the Garmin got too sweaty and slipped off. Once we discovered my heart rate could go quite high for my age, we could raise the heart rate zones a little, although we did not actually write this down. We trained on heart rate for sure, but did not refer to them as being in zones very often.

In Ironman race, maximum of six energy bars, probably less. Pour water on head and arms to stay cool, and drink loads

Nick's shoes weigh 200 grams racing and 280 grams training
Nick recommends 300 grams racing and 340 grams training for me, as I am 6ft 3 ½ and Nick is quite a bit shorter.

TRAINING PERFORMANCE:

Recovery Week - Starting 13th August

Drop intensity. Recovery week.

Monday: 35-min run, 2.7 miles.
Tuesday: 37.5-min run, 3 miles
Swim – 39 minutes, 30 lengths. I would have been using pull buoy here almost certainly, to help me get better body position, as my front crawl was abysmal when I started.
Wednesday: 45-min run, 3.5 miles
Thursday: 1hr bike
Friday: Swim 30 lengths - 45 minutes (breathing both sides).
5k run on treadmill, 23 minutes 40 seconds. Nick had told me to do a 35-minute easy run on the road, but it was pouring down with rain and I could not resist seeing how quick I could go on the treadmill. That was 35 seconds quicker than last time, so I'll take it.
1hr 30min building core strength, weights and stretching
(6hr 24m).

Chilham Castle Duathlon October 2012 - race strategy and preparation. This would be my first race. My coach, Nick, is the defending champion. It's a 10km run, 40km run and a 5km bike ride. Nick also holds the record time at 2hrs 8 minutes. The run is cross-country. Very hilly, up and down, with more ups than downs. The first half of the bike is quite hilly and the second half of the bike is quite flat and fast.

Check registration:
- Pack bags Friday morning with plenty of time to spare, as the race is very early Sunday morning.
- Charge Garmin watch.
- Friday - tape Electrolyte drinks to the frame on my bike. Tape them so they stay on, but are easy to pull off. Fold back the end so it's easy to pull off. Thank God for Nick showing me all the tricks of the trade. There are so many things to learn.
- Pack - Trainers, socks, three run gels, two power bars, pump, heart rate monitor.
- Sonia coffee flask Sat morning. This is more nutrition than Nick recommends, but I'd rather take too much than too little on my first race.

The times I set in my head before Chilham Castle Duathlon October 2012:

10km, 54mins, 6.2 miles (1hr easy)
40km, 1hr 20mins bike, 24.8 miles (1hr 30mins easy)
5k, 26mins, 3.1 miles (30mins easy)
2hr 40m did not include transitions. Whoops.

Nick's course record for Chilham is 2.08.37

Warrens 40km bike time was 1hr 4min. Warren is my neighbour and friend. He is in his third year of cycling and is quite into it. He's pretty athletic, as he used to compete for England at Gymnastics. He's a good person to go out on a ride with and measure my progress against.

Run course - first 1.5km mostly uphill then downhill.
Then big uphill and gradual uphill until the end.
5km laps.

Bike course - most of first 20km uphill - two main climbs, then next 20km some downhill and flat.

My strategy - go at 155 heart rate. Up to 165 heart rate up hills.

General Brainstorming
Here, I would put down my thoughts every day. There is a lot of information to take in when taking up Triathlon for the first time and training for the Ironman.

Swim tips
- Think "kick with thighs" – I definitely did do this a lot.
- Lie on sofa back and kick up – never did this, actually.
- Lie on bed and practice swim stroke – never did this either actually, but sounded good at the time. Must have read it somewhere, or Nick may have suggested it.

Other races:
One a month from March – I think Nick suggested once a fortnight in the beginning. Not sure if this will be practical with my two young children and business commitments, but will do the best I can and maintain life balance.

- Laborn lake swim, Brighton – never got round to doing this
- Tooting Lido – never used this either
- Brockwell Lido – eventually did this about six weeks before the Ironman and tried out my wetsuit for the first time. Good job I did,

as putting the wetsuit on and off was harder than the actual swimming.

To clean bike:
WD-40, Teflon lube on chain, Halfords. Wiggle – never used any of these. Got my cleaner to clean my bike after my races for an extra £5, Nick to clean bike when paid him for fixing something else and bike mechanic in Crystal Palace shop or in Klagenfurt to do it.

Bike 112 miles
112 by 5 is 22.4 average speed
112 by 5 1/2 is 20.36 average speed
112 by 6 is 18.66 average speed

Anything quicker than six hours seems really hard to deliver, although I do hear that the roads are fast in Klagenfurt. I'll just try not to think about the two big climbs, and kind of blank them out for now. I'll dream on and try my visualisations. Keep thinking about aero wheels, but do not feel I have good enough control of the bike yet, especially on downhill slopes, so want to improve that and ride safely. Rome wasn't built in a day, and neither were Chris Lieto's or Jurgen Zack's bike strengths.

Between the 20th of August and 23rd of September 2012, I had a bit of a challenge away from the training. I know I spent thirteen days at Seminars, so it would have been a lot on the turbo, not much swimming and lots of running. Swimming front crawl with pull buoy for sure. Some runs in the dark for sure.

One of the Seminars was a 7-day NLP Seminar with Richard Bandler. I managed to get on stage a few times to get hypnotised, and during timeline hypnosis I managed to visualise finishing the Ironman, which was an awesome experience. I had to visualise whatever I wanted before I achieved something and then afterwards, then see it as a movie and play it backwards and forwards, etc.... I had to incorporate all the senses into it to make it more real, and it was a pretty strong feeling and image, which I can still recall over a year later.

I think I must have bought my turbo around this time as well. Nick recommended a Tacx Turbo Trainer. I bought one on Amazon for around £250. That was about £50 off. They are quite expensive, but really good, as you can see your power, mileage and RPM, they have many different gradients, they give you a really good work out and they're not too noisy. They are a lifeline if you live in the UK, as they enable you to get your base bike miles in during the winter as well.

Week 12 of Ironman Training

Recovery week was ending 30th September. Was 6hrs 15mins - then one more recovery week starting 30th Sept - 3-day seminar in second week; first week I was over tired. I guess my body needs to get used to this amount of training still, and my swim and running techniques are not lowering my fatigue.

Sunday September 30th
Monday: 50-min run, 5 miles
10-min swim, 500 metres – must have been tired here to pull out of the swim so quickly, or sore left knee most likely and then deep heat gel when I got home.
Tuesday: 1hr 15-min bike, 22 miles – includes traffic lights and traffic getting in the way, so I must be faster. Every psychological edge helps. God, this Ironman training is tough. I've told so many people about it now that I have to follow through with it.
Wednesday: 40-min run
Thursday: 60-min run, 5.83 miles; 40-min swim, 1600 metres (32 lengths).
Friday: Day off
Saturday: Day off
(4hr 30mins total)

October 3rd – my weight is down to 81.9 kilos; that's 12st 12lbs

Sunday 7th October
Sunday: 40-min run, 4 miles
Monday: 50-min run, 5.3 miles; bike 1hr 35mins to mountain climbs cadence.
Tuesday: Fitness test, 30-min bike, 9.2 miles. Run 30mins, 3.2miles; 40-min bike.
Wednesday: Day off
Thursday: Swimming lesson - 30 minutes, 15 lengths. Then 1500 metres in 45 minutes.
Friday: 30-min run, 3.2miles

14 October
Sunday: Day off
Monday: 1hr bike, about 16 miles
Tuesday: 32-min run, 3.2 miles; 34-min run, 3.35 miles
Wednesday: Swam 1km in 24 minutes. 23 miles in 1hr 20mins
Thursday: 40-min run - 5k in 26mins. 10mins core.
Friday: Day off
Saturday: 20-min spin on turbo
Sunday 2hr 53mins, first ever race, came 46th out of 112 people

Several days before the Chilham Castle Duathlon, I was really looking forward to it. As it led up to it, I felt a sense of great anticipation and lots of nerves. It was great that Nick was going to pick me up early in the morning on race day in his van and we were going to go down together; I could pick Nick's brains along the way. He was the defending champion as well, so I was in the best possible hands.

The race started at 8.15am, and Nick must have picked me up at around 5.40am, as it was over an hour's drive. It had been pouring down with rain all week, and as we drove down, it was pouring down in the dark. My head wandered off to the Ironman racing in the sun that I had seen on YouTube and on television. What a mug I am, racing in England, I said to myself, then at the same time, I had this thought – *Well, it will make me tougher for Klagenfurt Ironman, and I'll see what I'm made of.* Nick had told me I'd done the training. That gave me more confidence. I had a flask of really strong coffee on the way down. I thought I would need a big caffeine boost, especially in my first ever race as an adult, and hoped that I could clean my system out by going to the toilet a few minutes before the race. I was thirty-seven years old and a newbie to Duathlon.

We arrived fairly early, probably around an hour before the race started. We went straight over to get our goodie bags containing a free T-shirt and race equipment - a timing chip to put on our ankle and a race number to wear with safety pins. I did not have a running belt, which is definitely a bit easier to put on, so I suggest you get one. A running belt can be worn on the front of the run and then just turned around on the bike and turned around again for the second run. Whereas if you have your number safety-pinned, it gets confusing, as you can rip the number quite easily, so it hangs off, and you have to wear your number on the front on the runs and on your lower back on the bike. Then there were stickers for the side of the bike and the front of the bike helmet. Also, there was a sticker on the frame of the bike. The timing chip is really important, as without it you do not get an official time and position, and you have to pay for it if you lose it. It goes on your left ankle, usually on the outside, away from the pedal on the bike.

Nick got his entire kit ready in a flash, as I kept faffing around and procrastinating. I was asking him a million questions. He was getting more and more focused on the race, and said less, just saying "you've done the training" and "relax". I managed to go to the toilet and relieve myself, so I was a bit lighter, and then there was the race briefing. It was cold, wet and windy. The ground was soaking wet and muddy, and my shoes were getting filthy on the grass in the field.

We put our bikes into transition. Nick was really slick, and I was faffing around, thinking, *Am I going to put a jacket on when I get on the bike, or not?* and looking at what gels to have at the start of the second run. I had two drinks bottles full and two power bars taped to the frame of my bike. Nick said it was too much food to have, but the race seemed like a long way and I did not want to do the dreaded bonk that I had heard my cycling friend and neighbour Warren talk about. He said he had it once, and he hadn't been able to move and had felt like crying, or had cried. I kind of blanked that out. Warren was super-fit as well, so for him to say that made me kind of switch off and think, *I am always going to take loads of nutrition in.* Better too much than too little, or so I thought at that time in my swim, bike, run career.

A few minutes before the start, Nick started racing around. He was warming up. His warming up looked quicker than my race pace. I panicked as I saw that I had left my gel in the car. Nick said I did not need it anyway, as it was meant to be drunk with water and I had never used one before, so not the time to try now. That wasted a bit more of my nervous energy, and even if I had gone back to get it, then I would have probably missed the start by 30 seconds, and would have been exhausted running 300 metres downhill and uphill again back to the car. Nick had said before to run at my planned heart rate pace and then watch him slowly run away. The idea was to run my own race and go for the time I had laid out for myself.

The start was really exciting. There were around 120 people in the race. There was a big countdown from 10-0. It was pouring down with rain. With about five seconds to go, I gave off a massive "woohooooooo". I had positioned myself about three rows from the front. There must have been about fifteen rows of eight people. Then 5,4,3,2 and 1. Go.

There was a big hooter sound and then the sound of hundreds of feet squelching quickly through the mud. I started off pretty quickly. After a minute or two, I realised my heart rate was about 20 beats quicker than my planned pace and I was running a lot quicker mile place than I planned, so I eased off a bit and there were less athletes around me. I'd started off quite quickly, so every few seconds an athlete would come up to me. Each time this happened, I would look at my heart rate and stick to my race pace and my own race plan. About a minute into the race, the mud became so thick for the next mile that people were slipping everywhere. Some people were going straight through the middle. I now know that most of these were probably wearing cross-country trainers with grips, probably Saucony's. (This is something that Nick advised me to do when I ran the same race a year later, and I ended up with a much better result.) I was wearing Asics that were slipping all over the place. However I have size 12 feet, which must have helped me balance better than a lot of the other competitors, and had tied my trainers up really tightly, which turned out to be a great move. I saw at least 10 people lose one of their trainers and have to stop in the mud to put it back on. I saw one woman lose one of her shoes twice. Soon enough she burned past me again. It was one of Nick's friends, who he had introduced to me before the race.

It was all uphill for the first mile and a bit, then a few hundred metres downhill, and then a massive downhill with an aid station at 2.5km. I found that during the first mile, everyone was kind of getting into their destined position, almost, then after that I tended to catch people up on the downhill slopes and lose ground on the same people on the uphill slopes. Nick said this was largely due to my power to weight ratio and was similar for cycling up and down hill as well.

At the first aid station, I probably had some water and an isotonic drink. I was set on over-fuelling and not bonking. After the 2.5km aid station, the course was flat for 10 metres and then there was a massive uphill slope. It's quite tough psychologically, as the whole time you are going downhill you know you are going to have to go straight back up the other side. That part of the course was all grass, and was less slippery than the mud fest of the first mile. Then there was an uphill slope, but half-muddy half-grass for a few hundred metres, and turn the corner and it was uphill again. *That's going to hurt at the end,* I was thinking.

Prior to the race, I just wanted to finish in the top half. I was sure I was in the top half throughout the first run, and had my strength, the bike, to come. The question was, could I ride around safely, and could I hold it together for the second run? Also, would I ever get out of transition, as I had brought so many things to it and not made my mind up about what I was going to put on and take?

Then we were back to the start, and under the finish banner. That was 5km and the first lap done. Sweet…. Another aid station … I probably took one small glass of water and one small glass of tonic. There were quite a few people cheering us by now, which was an awesome feeling. It made the pain worth it, the training worthwhile and was good for the ego … whoops, I mean soul.…

Second time around the muddy mile, and I was more running over branches of fallen trees around the side. It was a bit like hop, skip and jump at times. I was doing quite well through the muddy bit. The race had thinned out a bit. I was hitting my target of doing the first 10km in less than 54 minutes, which was good. My Garmin was working; I had it split into four data fields: Heart rate, time, distance in miles and pace per mile. I probably looked at it every 10 seconds, which is way too much, but helped me disassociate from the pain, I think.

I finished the first 10km in 53 minutes and 20 seconds, and gave a massive "wooohoooo" when the crowd was at its most congested, and then got to transition.

Transition. Right … where's my bike? … Where's my bike? I think I had to ask one of the Marshalls where my number was. I think I had gone a bit dizzy, as I was looking around on the opposite side in the opposite direction. Then it went something like this: shoes off, helmet on, shades on, can't see anything, shades off. Grab something to eat. No. Got enough on my bike. Right. I am cold. It looks like it's going to carry on raining. I'll put my jacket on and push the bike, and we're away. Oh, shades on again. Walking quickly … let's make it a jog. A few hundred metres until I can get on the bike … I'll overtake this guy. On the bike. Crazy downhill slope. Take shades off. This bit's dangerous, so bumpy … hey, someone's going past me … easy dangerous downhill bit … no-one's going past me on the bike unless they've got aero wheels on, or it's Nick lapping me. OK … right, we're off. OK, let's get those bike legs going. Feel OK … bit stiff. Let's pick people off.…

OK, so a few people must have gone past me in transition, but one of them had aero wheels so he doesn't count, and he had an aero helmet. I'll pick the others off. That guy's massive … how did he run quicker than me? Ah well, he can't ride up this hill very fast … God, in too high a gear … let's pace myself.… What this … more rain? Let's go at 80%-90%, comfortable power and go on feel. It's too dangerous to look at my watch that often. Let's go on feel.… Let's get some drink in now … ah, isotonic … yummy.… I'll still pick people off … ah, overtaken one person … now, number two … number three … have some drink … ah, number four … some more drink.… Change gear … that's better … keep this pace.… There are two ahead … I'll go past them both.… Ah, this bit is a bit steep … hey, he's gone away again … not going to let him get through that … let's put on some power … yes … got that one and the other…. Hey, she must be a fast runner … fair play…. Right, got through those two … who's my next victim? Let's have a drink … wooaoo, who was that? Ah, someone on aeros with an aero helmet … that was a Cervelo Time Trial Bike. Doesn't count … I'm still in the same position…. He must have lapped me … if not, it still doesn't count, as he's cheating on that thing…. Right, so overtaken six…. Right, let's try and keep up with this aero guy and follow the angles he's taking ... ah, he's going too fast … I need to pace myself…. Another group ahead…. Have a drink first … and some of this power bar … quick bite and in my shorts … another sip….

Now let's get past the group. One at a time … got past the first one… Slip in front and take a breather until I go past the next one…. Bit steeper than I thought, this bit…. I'll wait until the next flat bit and burn past a couple more….
Quick look at watch … on schedule … good…. Now the flat bit … let's burn past … passed one opponent … and another…. Flat now, let's get the power on and put on the power here … can feel my legs a bit, but let's go for it….

As the bike went on, I felt good. Took lots of fuel in. Finished the two bottles of drink and a power bar. Legs were not as powerful as normal on the bike, but that was understandable, as I'd already done a 10km run and a couple of climbs to start. I managed to keep it all together safely and held my position going into transition 2, or T2 as it's most commonly called. The last few hundred metres up to T2 are really steep. I came off the bike and jogged to my bike rack. I was pretty blown. It was quiet at the transition. The whole race was pretty spaced out. It looked like less than half the bikes were back, so I was pleased with my position and more pleased that there was only 5km to go. My legs felt really stiff. I spoke to one guy and laughed, saying something like:

"This is my first race and I am exhausted, and I am training for an Ironman in June."

The other guy laughed, and said, "Not me… NO way … you're crazy. Good luck with that. Have a good run."

I took a gel and started to jog off. My whole body was really stiff and I was tightened up. I was managing to run, but was definitely a lot slower than the first time around. My bike split was just under 1hr 25 minutes - about what I expected; a couple of minutes worse maybe, but it was quite hilly.

I managed to keep running round the final 5km. I ran 20 metres past the start and then had a massive pee that lasted for about two minutes. Two or three guys came past me, but I managed not to let anyone overtake me when I started running again. In fact, I caught one or two people up. The last kilometre was a killer. I was so stiff, and it was uphill. I passed one or two people and told them to "come on" and "carry on", but most of the time I had been running on my own. They said that they couldn't, and said "well done". I liked the friendliness of it all. With about 300 metres to go, I finally stopped jogging and started walking. Within three seconds, I saw Nick smiling and shouting encouragingly:

"Come on Jase, you're nearly there."

Talk about timing. Nick had already finished and was there taking pictures of me with his camera. I started running again, or more stumbling with a bit of a jog. I had only walked for about five seconds, and when I looked behind there was nobody within sight. So I pushed the final few hundred metres and could hear someone coming up behind me … pushed a bit further and held my position. I got over the finish line and they said my name, Jason Pegler, which was great. People cheering. I high-fived a few people and gave a big, "woowooooo" just before finishing…. As soon as I got over the line, someone put a medal round my neck, which was great, and I took a few isotonic drinks and some water. I think I had a few Jaffa Cakes and mini energy bars as well. Whatever was on offer, I took it, and felt a real sense of achievement. Oh my God, an Ironman was another 27.2 kilometres, more running, and 87 more miles running than what I'd just did in a couple of months training; oh, and I would have to swim 3.8km first as well, and swimming was my weakness. As I was full of endorphins from the race, it felt really doable though, and I felt like I was now in the game instead of just training or just talking about it. We left quite quickly afterwards, as Nick wanted to go. He'd not won this time around and had come 6th overall, only winning his age group and not the overall.

I was fairly pleased with my result. 46th overall, with a time of 2 hours, 53 minutes and 28 seconds. There had been 116 people in the race. I was in the top half of the field in each part of the race, but below average in both of the transitions. (I would enter the same race a year later as a much fitter athlete and with a much better time and position, but that's another story)

Chilham Castle 2012 Duathlon Time splits:

Average Speed

First 5km	00:26:29
Second 5km	00:27:18
T1	00:03:13
Bike	01:24:38
T2	00:01:58
Run 2	00:29:49

Sunday October 21st 2012

Easy week - did race on Sunday
Monday: Day off - go for a good walk to loosen stiffness
Tuesday: 30-min run, 3.2 miles
Wednesday: 30-min run, 3.2miles
Thursday: 30-min, 3.4 miles
Friday: 30-min, 3.2 miles
Saturday: Day off

Sunday: Day off
Monday: 1hr turbo, 17 miles (Two lots of 30mins)
Tuesday: 45-min run, 7.1km; 40-min swim, 1.7km
Wednesday: Turbo 1hr, 20.2mph av sp, av watts 200, 32km? (-1av). Swim 1.1km, 25mins
Thursday: Day off
Friday: 6.35-mile run, 1hr
Saturday: Run 5.45 miles, 50min
Sunday: Day off

5th November
Monday: 1hr swim, 2.5km; bike 1hr, 17.8miles
Tuesday: Run 50mins, 5.49 miles
Wednesday: 1hr swim, 2.5km
Thursday: 1hr bike, 20.1 miles, same average speed (gradient 0 all the way). 40-min run, 4.49miles
Friday: Day off
Saturday: Day off
3 runs, 40/50/60mins
1 tempo - (40mins: 10mins to park, 20mins sub 8, 10mins back)
60-min hill reps by Dom's old house - 4 hill climbs and back
50mins 3 – 15-m in warm up 3x miles at 7min/mile pace and back
2 swims - 1hr straight through, 1hr drills

3 turbos. +1 Gradient x 30mins, massive gear 60rpm, turbo, steady ride use +1 40mins, spins 105-110, 30mins

- YouTube "putting a wet suit on". Needs to be really tight. Wiggle. Try on with gloves on so don't rip it.
- Blueseventy Helix - £500
- Buy: tri bars

Sunday: 40-min bike (+1 12m 18mph 215 watts Avg)
Monday: 1.8km drills in 50mins (1km breathing left) 35-min bike +6 hard.
Tuesday: 5.18 miles, 4 hill reps, 46mins (walked up hill some of the time, first time ever walked in run session; average heart rate 166, maximum heart rate 188; average pace 8.57-min miles. Best pace 4.43-min mile, elevation gain 545 feet.
Wednesday: 30-min run, 5km in 23min, then 1hr core work in gym.
Thu: 30-min turbo 105-110 cadence+1 avs 18mph (easy gear)
Friday: 1hr swim, 2.5km
(5hr 51mins)

Would my body take a second Ironman in Bolton in August? My mind wants to, so my family can see me then.

Sun 16th November - run week, as I was at a Seminar, so could not swim or bike much.... I remember Nick told me to run 26 miles in 7 days, so I knew what it felt like. It was psychologically quite helpful and exciting to do something a bit different.

Sun-Tue road. Wed-Friday treadmill.
Sunday: 7.11 miles, 63mins
Monday: 4.32 miles, 34mins
Tuesday: 5.26 miles in 45mins
Wednesday: 3.26 miles, 24mins (treadmill), plus 45mins gym strengthening and work out.
Thursday 3 miles, 25mins
Friday: 3.2 miles, 25mins
Total distance ran this week – 26.13 miles
(3hr 36mins)
Sat off, Sun off

Week starting 19th November:
Monday: Bike 30mins, 60-min swim with pull buoy.
Tuesday: Swim 60mins, sets of 500 metres, drafting Nick 3000 metres total

Wednesday: Bike 45mins turbo, 15-min WU (warm up), 4 x 5-min hard efforts at 260 watts at +1gradient, 10-15-min WD (warm down)

Thursday: Run 50mins - as 15mins WU, 20mins tempo (hr. 165), 15mins WD. Run to Crystal Palace Park 15mins - do 20mins temp effort on the bike loop we used, then WD 10-15mins easy home.

Friday: Bike 50mins - at high cadence +100 revs at 0 gradient, 5-min WU, then start at minimum 100rpm for 45mins (can go faster in last 5mins if you can)

Saturday: Rest day, family

Sunday: Run 90mins - LSD (long slow distance) HR (heart rate) 145

Here is a text from Nick in November 2012:

"Well done today your swimming has improved 60% watch the YouTube clips on second email for some more practical tips.

For your next few swims work on the 3 areas we discussed for max gains:

Pointing your toes, kick from the hips … getting rid of the parachute behind you."

Achieving just enough roll … by fingertip dragging drill … when you master this, do the same in full stroke, but don't quite touch the water with fingertips … this will then be perfect amount of roll.

Better 'catch'… after sliding arm into the water, 'dig' your hand down to catch the water, and pull over a barrel with a bent arm (90degree).

Finally, finish the stroke off at the back with a flip … thumb brushes your own thigh as it exits.

Week starting 26th November:

Monday: 60-min swim, using pull buoy

Tuesday: 50mins turbo 200-260w … 1hr gym core and stretch

Wednesday: Turbo as instructed.

Thursday: Run 5.16 miles in 50mins

Friday: 50mins turbo as instructed

Saturday: Rest

Sunday: Rest

Week 2nd of December:

Monday: 7.6 miles in 73 minutes

Tuesday: 9.23 miles in 90 minutes - elevation 471ft. Avg heart rate 149bpm, max heart rate 178bpm. Av mile 9.5mins.

Wednesday: Bike 45mins- Fast Cadence, 15-min Spin at 95rpm , 15-min Spin at 100rpm, 15-min Spin at 105rpm - av sp 18.8mph.

Thu: Turbo 1 of day, 60min bike plus 1 diff gears, Avg heart rate only 130 - Avg 18.1. (Turbo 2 of day - 45mins +6 Avg heart rate is 133. Run hill x5 reps Dulwich was 5.82 miles in 53mins (took extra half mile to get there) in dark and rain, quite pleased, Avg HR 155 top HR 180

366 minutes (6hrs 6m)

For a hard week:
Monday: Session 1 – Swim - 60mins - (2500m) - 50 lengths Time Trial (record your precise time). Almost certainly still using pull buoy here, as I needed to get my body position correct.
Wednesday: Session 5 - Swim 60mins - Drills and Swim – 100 metres swim full stroke, 100 metres Pull (one arm in front, pull with other arm), 100 metres full stroke , 100 metres pull (same as before but opposite arm out in front), 100 metres full stroke…. Repeat this five times. If arms can't do this, then alternate 100 metres full stroke with 100 metres with pull buoy. Stretching/Core- own design
Friday: Run 60mins, 20-min WU, 20mins tempo at 7-7.30 min/mile pace, 20-min WD
Bike on turbo at gradient +1, going up and down the gears on rear cassette. 5mins in each.
60mins.

For a medium week:
Thursday: Do a short blast session, 20 minutes on bike at threshold … 200-220 watts. Then immediately run 20 minutes hard pace, fast up to Crystal Palace Park, round our first bike loop and home, all at threshold. Hard because you're pushing … easy because it's all over in 40 minutes.
Wednesday: Maybe a visit to the pool? Do a 10-length easy warm up. Then do 100-metre reps x 10, trying to hold a time of 2 minutes per 100m. Check the wall clock. Set off every 2mins 30 seconds on next rep (so after your 2-min swim you get 30 seconds rest)

Week 9th December:
Sunday: 13.17 miles in 2hrs exactly.
Monday: 1hr turbo, 18 miles (+1 and 0)
Tuesday: Day off
Wednesday: 2.5km Swim in 1hr
Thursday: 20-min bike 200-225watts 20-min run flat out (had nasty fall at start of run)
Friday - Took day off
Saturday - Rest day

Three days off then:

Week beginning 16th of December:

Monday 16th December: Swam 3.8km in pool for first time. No pull buoy, obviously. Took 1hr 45mins (know I can do in 1hr 30mins - slower as less sleep last few days, stiff, bruises, but need to get it right).

Tuesday: Bike 40mins. Warm up 10mins at 90rpm. Grad +1 then increase 2 rpm every 5mins, until end.

Wednesday: Bike, long slow distance on road or turbo - 70mins, grad +1, 90 rpm, HR 140. Run 50mins, 'criss cross' session, take HR up to 160 and back down to 140 repeatedly. For whole 50mins.

Thursday: Short swim 20 x 50metres fast with 15 seconds rest. Took 24mins.

Short fast run round Crystal Palace Park, 3 miles.

(Did about 4 miles as swimming pool was closed)

Friday: Warm up, drills, then swim 6 x 200 metres in 4mins, 30 sec rest.

(Could not do, as swimming pool closed)

Sunday: Rest

Monday: Run 90mins … I remember doing some visualisations in the park and being very relieved that it was time to finally have some time off training.

REST OF WEEK OFF. XMAS! Yippee!!!!

Two weeks off from 23rd December - 6th of January.

Xmas email from Nick:

"Happy New Year Jase!

Take the rest. You will have 6 months solid training up to your race, when you start back on 7th.

First 12 weeks of BASE, steadily increasing the hours.

8 week BUILD.

4 week PEAK and TAPER.

Lots of work, so keep fresh now.

Cheers Nick."

Week January 6th 2013

Monday: 2-hr run 11.75miles

Tuesday: 40-min bike - heart rate up to 172. Av watts 235 approx av sp 21.5 approx. Felt a bit faint after 30mins; had a couple of sips of energy drink and finished off buzzing. Was it the run from yesterday, or having two weeks off training and coming back into it,

or a bit of both? Don't know. Swim 10 laps, 15mins, warm up, 20 laps 25m 5% above threshold, 15-second break per length....
Wednesday: 1hr run, 7.3 miles

Week January 13th 2013
Monday: Ran 6.7miles
Tuesday: Bike 227 watts average and ran 4.5 miles, swim 1.5km 15m 12m 11m splits
Wednesday: Bike 1hr, 23.5miles, top speed 33.4
Thursday: Run and gym
Friday: Swim 2.1km, 51mins, no pull buoy.

Training guide - 2 bike, 2 swim, 3 run - 5 days

January 18th - snowing, so flexible week, lots of bike on turbo:
Sunday: 40-min turbo. 13 miles on bike Avg w229.
Sunday: 30mins, 9.1miles on turbo
Monday: 18.5 miles in 1hr
Tuesday: 13.5 miles, 50mins, 19.6 Avg s
Wednesday: 7.6km in 45mins treadmill running.
Thursday: 60-min swim drills
Friday: 40-min run, av sp 9.5km 6.25km

Meeting with Nick.
Sharing every session on Google calendar now, so I can see in advance. To do list:
- Buy wetsuit
- Buy tri bars
- Enter races until big race

Week January 27th 2013:
Sunday: 100m run, 9.58 miles - treadmill 35-45 below max heart rate.
Monday: 45-min bike 12.2 miles; 40-min run at 146bpm
Tuesday: Bike 1hr, 18 miles
Wednesday: Yes, did calendar
Thursday: Swim 51mins, same as wed. (Did wrong session). Quicker than yesterday.
Friday: 40-min turbo at 100+ cadence

Whole of January 2013
Did every session, except one swim and one long run.

Cranleigh 21-mile run race:

Text from Nick:

"I think you need to have run at least a half marathon or 20 mile race and done a half Ironman before Austria. Cranleigh 21 to consider, if you prefer"

February 3rd
Sunday: Day off, cold
Monday: Day off, cold
Tuesday: Day off, cold
Wednesday: 7.26km, av sp 10.9km
Thursday: Swim 4 x 200 metres at 2mins 34sec to 2mins 40sec per 200 metres ... 40-min bike, 9.8miles +2 at end
Friday: 40-min bike, 11.7 miles, 18.6 av sp

February 10th
Sunday: 70-min run, 7.75 miles
Monday: 16.2 miles bike
Tuesday: 60-min swim, 45 lengths
Bike 60-min – 19.1 dist. ac av w 195
Wednesday: Run treadmill 10.39km in 1hr
Thursday: 45-min bike 13.4miles av sp 18, heart rate end 142. Then run (did not measure run distance, as reset wrong)

February 17th
Sunday: 105-min run, 16.18km
Monday: 50-min bike, 12.6 miles, av sp 15mph
Tuesday: l-hr bike
Friday: Run 64mins, 12.25km

February 24th
13.5-mile run in 130mins – I was pleased with this run. It was at a set heart rate. Below 170 I think, although I was allowed to speed up for the last 30 minutes.

March 3rd Spring BallBuster Duathlon – 8 mile run, 24-mile bike, 8 mile run:

The 3rd of March 2013 saw me compete in my second ever Duathlon. With my first Ironman looming in June 2013, I'd not done a triathlon yet, but would cross that road when I came to it, even if I had to limp over it. For anyone who has done the BallBuster, you know it's not a race for the faint-hearted.

It's an 8-mile run, followed by a 40-km bike ride, followed by an 8-mile run to finish. You have to complete the same 8-mile loop five times altogether, twice by running and three times on the bike. It's a very hilly course. The last mile of the run is up a really steep incline. That's hard enough on the first lap and on the bike, but on the last run it's a real energy-sapper.

This was the first race I'd ever travelled to before on my own. The previous week, I had done a test of the course with Nick. We'd gone out in the freezing cold. It was snowing on our way up there in Nick's van. We did two laps on the bike. I went out a bit hard on the first lap and was suffering a bit on the second lap. Then we put the bikes in the van and set out for a run. It had started snowing again. My feet, fingers and face had been freezing on the first few minutes on the bike, but gradually became numb, and then my body had heated up and got used to it. I'd missed a crucial turning on the bike, where Nick shouted at me to turn around and said not to do that in the race. On the run, I felt pretty good. I was relieved to have got off the bike. We were running pretty quickly together, and then, as we approached the last mile or so up the hill, Nick said he had to speed up, or he would get injured if he tried to run up hill too slowly. He disappeared into the distance around the corner, putting a couple of minutes on me. As I was nearing the top, he had walked back down and was urging me on to sprint as fast as I could. We'd done the 8-mile run in about 1hr 5mins, something like that. I thought I could go a bit quicker on race day, especially as I'd already done two laps on the bike. We put the bikes back in the van and put some warm gear on, then went to see Nick's friend, who owned a bike shop where we had parked the van.

We had some fruitcake, some water and a warm coffee. It was bliss to be inside, and I felt prepared for the BallBuster, or so I thought.

Come race day, I got there early. I was a lot fitter than I had been in October for my first race at Chilham, but I needed to be, as this was a more competitive field, a tougher course and a longer course. Nick had entered it several times before and came as high as 4th overall, in 2002. There were 290 competitors this time around.

I got there nice and early, parked my car and had my customary flask of coffee. It was good to get there early, as I needed the toilet and there was a big queue when I came out. I put all my gear in transition and spent an incredible amount of time faffing around with my transition gear etc....

There was a good atmosphere and a lot of people warming up. I wore a long-sleeved top, woolly hat, gloves and shorts. I saw one girl wearing just a short-sleeved top and shorts. It looked too cold for that. I was shivering before the start and I am a big guy, so she must have been absolutely freezing. I positioned myself near the front, about three rows back out of the thirty or so rows of people.

There was a really good atmosphere. A lot of people looked pretty fit and had all the gear, but who knows how much training they had done. We would find out soon enough. I gave my customary "woooohhoooooo" about 20 seconds before the start, and then ready, steady, go; we were off.

There was an incessant sound of rhythmic marching of feet running in unison. Incessant, as I knew there were going to be moments of pain and I knew it would be tough for me to get in the top half of this field in only my second race. I found that I was going pretty quickly. After a couple of minutes I looked at my heart rate and it was way over what I'd planned, so I eased off a bit. Then people gradually started over taking me. As the minutes went by, I found that I had secured an approximate position and kind of kept that placing. The odd person going past and myself over taking the odd person. I just kept looking at my watch every 20 seconds or so, to make sure I was bang on the heart rate and time I had set myself. I was more focused on heart rate than anything else, although the ego does get in the way a bit when you see people over taking you, so I was just pushing, if ever so slightly, harder than my heart rate suggested. I again found that I went quicker than others on the downhill slopes and slower than them on the uphill slopes. Was that because I had better technique and worse technique during those periods, or because of my power to weight ratio? God knows, but it was quite noticeable.

I remembered Nick saying, "On the downhill slopes, don't lose any time. Land on your toes more, or you are putting the brakes on." It did bang on my legs a bit, but seemed to improve my position a bit for the same effort, so it was a tactic that I was employing, and it meant I could hold back a bit and not make sure I overdid my heart rate on the above sections, which I was doing naturally whenever I looked at my Garmin.

After a couple of miles, the race really thinned out and there was a parade of athletes running on the quiet road. Quite a lot of people had overtaken me after the first mile, and people would continue to overtake me, but less and less as the miles went by. It was only 8.15 in the morning, so there was hardly any traffic, and we were in the middle of the countryside in the famous Box Hill, famous for Duathlons and well-known for being a tough cycle route for both newbie and more experienced cyclists. As the race went 4-6 miles I found my rhythm pretty well, and then for the uphill to finish the first

8 miles. I was glad that I'd done it with Nick the previous week. I took it easy-ish going up as my heart rate was high, and I probably over did it a bit, because I wanted to keep my position. I do not think anyone overtook me on the last mile going up.

I got to transition and finished my first 8 miles in a time I was pleased with. 61 minutes. My transition was pretty slow, as I took it easy and faffed around putting my jacket on. Still, part 1 was completed and I started to feel good.

My legs felt a little bit stiffer than I thought as I got onto the bike, and although I did overtake people, I was spinning in a gear that was one easier than I thought I would be using. I started drinking some electrolyte drink from my bottle. It was the lemon-flavoured PowerBar Isoactive Isotonic Sports Drink that was listed on the Ironman Klagenfurt website as being the official race drink, along with my vanilla power bars that were also the official power bars being used for Klagenfurt later in the summer. Feeling good with a bit of nutrition, I started picking people off.

I overtook quite a few people. One or two people, usually with Cervelos and aero wheels and aero helmets, would overtake me. Perhaps they were even lapping me. I managed to keep some of them in sight on the sharp downhill slopes, which proved helpful, as it helped me pick my lines better and I was still not really confident descending quickly. I did find that every time I went out on the road, I became more confident in my handling.

The bike was pretty tiring, and I had two full energy bottles and two power bars. This is more nutrition than Nick suggested, but I was still an inexperienced athlete and felt like I would rather have too much than too little, as I've usually got a pretty strong stomach.

The 24-mile bike leg took me 1hr 25 minutes. That was quite a bit longer than I thought it would take, although it was very hilly and I had already run 8 miles. By the time I got to T2, that's Transition 2, my legs were feeling really stiff and I must admit I was pretty exhausted. I told myself that I was not looking forward to the next 8 miles, which was not good sports psychology.

I was slow in transition. I had two gels in my hand. One I had tried in training a few times and one that I had been given as a freebie for the race. I decided to take neither and took a small Mars Bar with me instead. What a mistake that turned out to be. I was feeling really bad, but managed to run the first 2-3 miles a bit slower than I planned without really losing any places, then I felt worse all of a sudden. There were one or two aid stations, where I had some water, as I did not feel like any more isotonic. The water only seemed to help for a few seconds, and I started pouring it on my head, which seemed to help more than drinking it. I had discarded my beanie hat the second time around. In fact, within a mile of the first run I had taken it off and put it inside my trousers, as I was boiling. I had long craft trousers and top as well as gloves on and was probably too hot. Even though the temperature was really cold, I am 6ft 3 ½ and 85 kilos, so my body was pretty hard to cool down.

I took the Mars Bar about 4 miles in. I felt great for a couple of minutes, maybe 10 minutes in fact, and then - ahhhh. I thought back to eating a big Mars bar on the way down in the car at Chilham. I remember Nick did not say anything when I mentioned it. Were Mars Bars bad for racing? I thought a Mars Bar a day helped you work, rest and play. Later on I mentioned this to Nick, and he said something much more sophisticated and logical than I am about to write, but something like, "It gives you a buzz with the sugar and then you are more exhausted than before."

I was absolutely gone. I kept running, but my legs felt heavier and heavier. I also started to look back quite often. I could see one or two people quite a long way behind me, and they were gaining. Then I looked at my heart rate monitor; my mile pace; how many of the 8 miles to go - anything to try and keep me focused. I looked around again and could see a few more people behind, and they were even closer. Then I look at my heart rate monitor, pace, keep focusing on running. Then I could hear footsteps. One person came past ... a few more seconds looking at my watch ... and heart rate monitor ... wooden legs ... tummy ache.... I could hear more footsteps coming up from behind ... someone else overtaking....

I looked around nearly 7 miles into the 8 miles, and could see a massive group of around 40 people gaining....

Then someone in front of me, who I had been catching up, suddenly stopped and let out a massive sigh: "Ahhhhhhhh."

I was about 20 metres behind him.... Immediately, I stopped as well....*Oh no,* I thought.... I saw him walk for 10 seconds and then he started running again. I did exactly the same thing and thought I would try to catch him.... Then I could hear more footsteps, and someone else overtook me. I looked back, and the big group was gaining on me...

I was not gaining on the guy in front of me … then he stopped and started walking again … I ran an extra ten steps and stopped.… This scenario played out another three or four times, until the whole group of around 40 people had overtaken me in several minutes.… Then, eventually, I caught up with the guy in front, and said: "Come on, mate,"

"You go ahead, mate," he said. That spurred me on.

I got to the top of the hill and knew there were only around 400 metres left. I decided that nobody was going to overtake me again, and that I would try and catch a few people in front. I caught one or two and took one look back. There was a guy in a British Army jacket, who was coming up really fast. I thought, *There is no way I am letting anyone else overtake me.* I sprinted as fast as I could. It was as fast as I could go. I managed to get to the finish line and could hear him coming. There were quite a few people watching and saying, "come on", and a big finish line with an electronic clock in front. I managed to hold the guy off. However, 10 metres before the line, my legs completely seized up and I nearly fell over. I was absolutely exhausted, but managed to finish ahead of him.

My time for the second 8 miles was 1hr 13 minutes. That was 12 minutes slower than my first 8 mile run. Nick did say that the plan was to go the same pace on the first 8 miles as the last 8 miles, and the fact I had not done that had worsened my position and result. However, I was really happy to get over the line.

"Well done; I was trying to catch you, but couldn't," the army guy said, which was nice.

I was given a BallBuster hooded top, which I was really proud of and wore every day for a week afterwards. I had some recovery drinks and food straight at the end. I was so exhausted that I actually went in the ambulance, mainly to get more water, but also because it was warm, and just to check how I should stretch my legs, which had gone into a bit of a spasm. After drinking a couple of bottles of water in there and blagging some biscuits, I felt a bit embarrassed and then left. I went back to the car and got dressed and sat in the car for a bit, texting my girlfriend and my coach and probably my mum and dad as well. I just wanted to let them know that I had done it and that I was OK. I ate and drank in the car for a few minutes with the heater on and then went back to transition to get my bike and kit. By the time I got back to the car, the car park had cleared and I drove home. My calves were aching a bit on the way home when I used the accelerator and the brake, but as the minutes passed I felt a real sense of achievement, having completed my first Spring BallBuster.

I was less than four months away from Klagenfurt. My BallBuster race had taken me 3hrs 45 minutes. I had come 185th out of 302 people. Klagenfurt was only an extra 10 miles running, 88 miles on the bike, oh yes, and 2.4 miles of swimming, which was my first event. It would also be in really hot conditions, which was not meant to be good for big athletes like myself, but I had achieved another big stepping stone.

I spoke to Nick later in the day and we discussed what I did well and what I could have done better next time. I'd run the first 8 miles pretty well, but maybe too quickly, which had affected my bike and second run. I'd also got my nutrition wrong with the Mars Bar and maybe had too many power bars and too much isotonic, as I had stomach ache. There was plenty of time to get it right in training for later that summer in Klagenfurt. My next race would be 21 days later – the Cranleigh 21-mile run, when it would be snowing.

3rd March 2012 BallBuster Race splits:

Run 1: 8 miles 61mins
Bike 1: 24 miles 85mins
Run 2: 8 miles 7mins
6-min transitions
3hrs 45mins
185th out of 302.

I was a bit disappointed with my overall position and the way I had broken down towards the end, but happy to go so quick on the first 8 miles, ride the bike safely and beat quite a few people. I had hoped on getting in the top half of the field, but now knew what it would take next time around. It was also a good start to my spring training, with Ironman Klagenfurt less than four months away.

Swimming faster I hope:

I still had to keep my swimming going, and would constantly get advice from Nick and sometimes watch freestyle swim videos on YouTube.

Swim Technique notes:

Hands relaxed, swing hips, keep elbow touching body, rotate with hips, shoulder just below water when turning, not further … feel momentum before switching again, hands down just below elbow, not too far down. Keep shoulder up when doing each stroke ... elbow touching body ... not high....

High elbow means you can pull your body forward for longer on the stroke, and helps symmetry and continuum of school ... (Evans coaching). Position hand and forearm downward at same time. Develop good Tempo and symmetry ... left and right side virtually the same....
Bilateral breathing every three seconds.... Low intensity drills....

Pull with an 'S' shape.... 'S' shape the whole and finish on your bum. Pull all the way back with your shoulder, not just your forearm, which is a big mistake....

Ear on shoulder when breathing and cheek in the water

Reach
Catch
Pull
Push
Recovery

Pointed toes = more extended flipper

Small fast kick helps you keep hips on top, making you swim smoother

Look straight down at the bottom of the pool....

Bilateral breathing balances out strength of the body....

Training and Ironman Strategy Notes March-April 2013:

Week March 3rd – had BallBuster race and took a few days off to recover.

Hi Nick, done all sessions so far this week. Swim warm up and down, plus 40mins, 30 x 50 metres, 1500 metres
40-min run treadmill, 6.64km, went on feel exhausted straight after swim. All four sessions between 3.00pm yesterday and 11.00am today. Great to eat straight after in cafe :)
Friday, first 2hr turbo. 33.9 miles

March training notes:

Rotation drills YouTube (from hip body as one)
Swing from hip
Swim downhill to raise legs
Head higher to raise hips.

Planning some long bike rides to build bike endurance:
Sunday 7 April - 50 and/or 80-100 miles on bike ride

April 11th,12th or 14th - Warren 50-mile bike

Klagenfurt Adjustment Estimate:
Swim: 1hr 45mins
Bike: 5hr 45mins
Run: 4hr 30mins
Transitions: 10mins
12hr 10mins

Maximuscle Cyclone - protein - buy Creatine in May/June

Spearing arm at top of water not too stretched – fingers

Wednesday 15th March: 13.80m 13.25km
Thursday March 14th - swim breakthrough 2km in 44m 5sec

Thursday 17th March: Bike, Warren
3hrs 14mins 43.42 miles...
Average heart rate 127bpm. Max 176. Av speed
13.4, very hilly.

March 21st - Swim Pyramid:
400 metres 11mins 09s
200 metres 5mins 48 and 5mins 35
100 metres x 4 = 2mins 40 - 2mins 49
50 metres x 8 = 1mins 11 - 1mins 18

Cranleigh possible times and positions from 2012:
2hr 59mins gets 275th
3hr 15mins = 390th
3hr 30mins = 496th

March 24th 2013 - Cranleigh 21-mile race:

Cranleigh strategy:
Cranleigh HR should be 160-170. Do first loop at 160, then allowed to go up towards 170 on second smaller loop, after 15-milers finish and you continue through to 21.

So, just 21 days after the BallBuster, I entered my third race in my run up to Ironman Klagenfurt 2012. On Sunday morning, March 24th 2013, it was the Cranleigh 21 mile run. There were nearly 1,000 runners. One-third would stop at 15 miles and around two-thirds would go the full distance. It was an early morning start and a bit of a drive, so I had a good helping of organic porridge and a coffee for breakfast. Then I took my customary coffee mug with me.

There were two things on my mind race morning. The first was what to wear, as it had been snowing on and off the days before and also started to snow on race morning. I had been too warm in my kit at the BallBuster, so did not want to make the same mistake again. For the Cranleigh 21-miler I decided to wear a long-sleeved top - but a bit thinner than the one I wore at the BallBuster - Nike racing shorts, my compression socks, which I had become quite attached to, and an orange beanie hat.

The other thing on my mind was that I was determined to run, or at least jog, the whole race. I had failed to do this in both Chilham and the BallBuster, where I'd ended up walking, if only for about twenty seconds at Chilham, but on and off for at least a couple of minutes, or more like five minutes, at the BallBuster.

The other thing on my mind, although I tried not to think about it, was whether my knee would ache or not during the race. I'd had quite a few aches over the previous six months training. I was not sure whether it was my running technique, swim technique or just not being used to training so much that had caused it. It was most painful after running on the concrete, and sometimes I would have to run on the grass or on the treadmill instead. Quite often I would use the pull buoy when swimming instead of swimming naturally, as I could also feel it when swimming.

I used to raise my legs after sessions and lie on the sofa sometimes, as I read that this can help recovery. I would also take Ibuprofen tablets when it hurt or before bed, or even rub Ibuprofen gel on it or spray Deep Heat. I did find that the more I thought about it the worse it seemed to get, so often tried to blank it out. I rested it every now and then and sometimes had to ease off a bit as well, even if only 10% on my turbo sessions.

I would say I had completed 85-90% of the sessions Nick had set me from when I'd started in July. I'd skipped swimming the most, the odd bike and the odd run.

Anyway, back to Cranleigh, my first 21-mile race and the longest I had ever run in one go. I parked right next to the church hall where we had to register, which was very convenient, and after registering and using the toilet, got changed in the leisure centre opposite. Registration was simple. No transition area, no bike to take in. Just a number to put on. Even I could do that fairly quickly. The hardest decision to make was when to go to the start line, as it was freezing. I went back in the car for a minute or two and then started pacing around the church hall. Then there were only about five minutes to go, so I went to the start line and put on my Garmin belt, nearly forgetting the strap at the last minute, which would have made the watch useless for measuring my heart rate. By now I had upgraded from a Garmin 110 to a Garmin 910.

I got to the start line and it was very narrow and packed. In fact, I was right at the back. I was a few hundred metres from what turned out to be the front. I walked through a few rows of people, but did not feel like going to the front. *I'm pacing myself here,* I thought, *so I'll start off easy.*

I'd watched the previous year's start on YouTube, so knew it was quite packed at the beginning. The start was slower than I thought. I could not move at all for 30 seconds and had to jog way slower than normal for the first 3 minutes. The atmosphere was good. I could see people from running clubs running together. A lot of people had been chatting to each other before the start, and there were one or two comments of camaraderie and good luck as the race began. People were cracking jokes about how nice the weather was, as snow came lightly down on all of us.

By 3-4 minutes in, however, the race was well underway. I was catching some people up and being overtaken by others; mostly catching people up, as I had started about two-thirds of the way back. As each minute went by, it thinned out even more, and as I looked at my Garmin I started settling on my pace. Nick had set me a very specific heart rate.

Cranleigh HR should be 160-170. Do first loop at 160 (first 9 miles) then allowed to go up towards 170 on second smaller loop (9-15 miles) after 15 miles finish and you continue through to 21.

I realised a few days after the race that I had not remembered what Nick said, and had gone from 165 and up to 175 on the first loop. I think that would have affected my performance, but let's see what happened.

My focus was on watching my heart rate and also running each mile under 9 minutes. That would bring me a time of under 3 hours 9 minutes. Before the race, I thought I was capable of going under 3 hours, but knew if I did that it would really hurt. I knew I could do 3hrs 15mins, and knew I could easily go under 3hrs 30mins. The big question was how much pain I was prepared to put myself through in order to get the time I wanted, and whether or not my body would cope with what my mind was telling it.

I started off pretty well and felt good. I decided to run with three energy gels during the race and take the first one after 10km and then the other two when I needed them. I'd seen Chrissie Wellington and a few other pros in Ironman run with gels, and Nick said it wasn't a bad idea. I couldn't fathom out where to put the gels on my body, and they were too big for my shorts. Nick said using a running belt would slow me down. He said carrying gels was OK, as it would stop my fingers and wrists from going to soft when running.

There were about two aid stations on each lap. The first lap was 9 miles and then the second and third laps were 6 miles each.

I started off with each mile going under 9 minutes a mile. I had to put a bit of an injection of pace towards the end of the first mile, as I had been walking for the first minute or so. It was quite easy to go under 9 minutes for the first 5 or 6 miles, then it got a bit more difficult. I was working out in my head how many seconds below 9 minutes I was each mile, so felt confident I could go under 3 hours 9 minute pace. I would not allow my heart rate to go above 175. If it did, I made sure I eased off. Nick had said to keep it under 170 on the first loop of 9 miles, not 175, and I did not realise I had made that mistake until after the race. I took my time at each aid station, having a glass of water and a glass of isotonic, and then away I went, rejuvenated.

The later in the race an aid station came, the less of a positive impact it made. By the last couple I could only stomach water, and was then just pouring a bit over my head to cool my body down, making sure it did not go into my socks, as I did not want blisters.

I went through 10km spot on in around 54 minutes. I had my first gel and it gave me a good boost. The ground was quite undulating; small downhill slopes and then small uphill slopes. It never seemed flat for that long. I found myself gaining on people on the downhill slopes and losing ground a bit on the uphill slopes, but overall my position was pretty steady from miles 4-8. Then, around mile 8, I felt a sharp pain in my dreaded knee. *Oh no,* I thought, *not again.* I tried to not let it get me down and decided to shorten my stride a little bit and put the pressure more on the right side of my body. I tried landing on my right toe a bit more and it seemed to work. In fact, after five minutes the pain went away and I never felt it again during the race.

I had given myself a lot of positive self-talk, and it had done the job. It was getting harder to maintain sub 9 minute mile pace and now I had the uphill section. I decided there and then that I would not try and go under 3 hours, but would be happy with 3hrs 15mins. Psychologically, that made a big difference. It made me realise that I could run the entire race, and made me think there was no way I was going to blow or bonk. If I had aimed for less than 3 hours, then I think I would have bonked. I just wasn't fast enough and didn't quite have a good enough running technique or competitive edge at that time. Also, this was only a B race, as my A race was Klagenfurt, I told myself. It actually made me enjoy the race more at the time, as it was less painful. Not sure my ego liked it that much, but I was still proud of what I was achieving.

So now, instead of trying to go under 9 minutes every mile, I was calculating how far I'd gone and what speed I needed to go at. I had my second gel sooner that I'd planned, exactly 30 minutes after I had done the 10k, and then held onto gel number three for another 30 minutes. Each time, the gel seemed to have less impact than the one before. Not surprising really, as I was approaching the furthest I had ever run without getting on a bike in between and I still had another 6 miles to go.

We ran through the town centre once on each lap, and this gave everyone a lift. The Marshalls were really encouraging, and I took jelly babies when they were on offer, but only one or two at a time. I could see that some people were running together and talking about ultra marathons they were going to do or about how this was a warm up to London Marathon. The runners were friendly and the event was very well-organised. It was obvious where to run.

As I approached the end of lap two, I could see the finish line for the 15-milers. There was no way I was stopping there; I was determined to carry on. As each minute went past, my legs were getting heavier and my heart rate seemed to be getting higher, whilst I was trying to run at the same speed. I notice that between the 14- and 15-mile mark that around 30 people overtook me. I was holding back, as Nick said, to keep my heart rate down until the last 6 miles, then push it up a bit more. Some of the people that overtook me around mile 14 were really going for it, giving the last big push to finish the 15mile event.

From miles 15 to 21, I overtook some of the people that had overtaken me, overtook a few more and got overtaken by a few others. I was chatting to people every now and then, saying that this was the longest I had ever run and I was training for an Ironman. The other racers were really friendly. Lots of them were training for the London Marathon, one or two of them had done an Ironman before as well and quite a few had done a triathlon or some Duathlons. Most of them I spoke to had done a marathon before, and some of them had no doubt done loads, although I expect they were way ahead of me.

I felt good psychology at mile 16, and then each mile got harder and I got a bit slower, but I was getting happier as I was nearing the finish. By the time the last half a mile came around I was determined that nobody was going to go past me, and nobody did. I turned off the main road and into the finishing straight. There were quite a few people applauding, and I saw a woman in front of me who was in the distance. I raced as fast as I could to overtake her and then realised that she was finishing the 15-mile race. My legs turned to jelly and I knew someone was chasing really fast behind me as well, but I just managed to hold them off.

It was a great feeling. I got over the finishing line and then was given my Cranleigh medal straight away, which I was really pleased about. I had promised my son Oscar, who had just turned five, and my daughter Anna, who was nearly three, that they could wear it when I got home.

The 9-6-6 helped the mental countdown. A special thank you to the volunteer who shouted before the last killer hill (at mile 20!): "One last hill and then it's all downhill to the finish!" I may not have made it up that hill and kept running the whole way without that mantra in my head!

Then it was back to the village hall for a cup of tea and some homemade cakes. The cakes were lovely and tiny, so I had half a dozen of them. It was nice to be in the warm. I had a 15-minute massage for free, which did seem to help. I was really stiff and aching all over, but was definitely not injured, which was a big plus.

Below is a summary of my Garmin data from the race, which I uploaded onto Garmin Connect.

Distance: 21.2 miles. Average heart rate: 170. Maximum heart rate: 236 – that bit was a mistake, maybe due to not sweating or the cold weather at the start; it would have been around 193. Calories: 3139 (so it was OK to have the cakes). Best speed: 6 minutes 13 seconds (that would have been my sprint finish). Average pace: 9 minutes 17 seconds (would have been better if I hadn't had to wait the first 30 seconds and walk the next 90 seconds because of where I positioned myself near the back – everyone can go quicker right?!) Elevation gain: 794 feet – it was definitely an undulating course. Total time: 3 hours, 16 minutes and 51 seconds.

I had come 393rd out of the 589 people who did the 21-mile race, with an official time of 3hrs 16 minutes and 24 seconds, and would have been in the top half of the 15-mile racers.

After Cranleigh, I phoned Nick and discussed the race. He was really pleased and said it was a good stepping-stone for Klagenfurt. We discussed what I did well and what I could do better next time. I thought I had worn the correct clothes. The gloves had helped, and I was glad I did not have long trousers on, as I think I would have got too hot. I was really pleased to have run the whole way round. I had got my heart rate wrong by 5 beats per minute, which made me go anaerobic too early, so would pay more attention to that next time. Overall it was a pleasing result, and on to the next part of the training for Austria.

Swim Faster Please

By the end of March, my biggest fear was my swimming. I knew I could swim the Ironman distance, as I had done it in the pool, but I feared that it would aggravate my knee whenever I did front crawl and also worried that I was wasting so much energy during the swim and time that it would affect my Ironman bike and run times. My worst fear was that a really uneconomical swim would even damage my dream of finishing Klagenfurt.

So, Nick recommended that I went to see Dan Bullock. I saw him twice, once in March and once in April. Dan is a very experienced swim coach and runs Swim For Tri. He has also done a couple of Ironman's, and told me he had a lot of clients who had done Ironman's and were still doing them. That put me at ease straight away. I went over to Shoreditch to go and meet Dan the swim man.

The training pool was 25 metres and the darkest pool I had ever seen. Dan sounded like he had a PhD in swimming. He knew everything about it. He asked me to do 400 metres to warm up and explained that he would video me. When we watched it back, I could not believe how bad I looked swimming. It was so embarrassing. I was all ears. Dan then proceeded to talk for five minutes about everything that was wrong and what to improve to make it better. Then swim for a couple more minutes and some more feedback.... Then a drill and some more feedback.... Then another drill to do such and such and some more feedback. By the time the hour was up, I was absolutely exhausted and could feel my left knee again.

Dan Bullock's tips:

-   Dan said I needed to strengthen my core and mobility every day – I did this pretty well for around eight weeks, but then started to feel so tired during the training that I stopped doing it for half of the days in May and stopped completely in June, for fear of burning myself out.

-   Fins to help mobilise – nice in theory, but when I put them on in Crystal Palace pool they would not let me use them, as it was against health and safety, so only used them once.

-   Feel the big toes brushing to stop them splaying too far apart – I concentrated on this quite a lot and it did seem to work.

- Tiny movement at the hip generates all you need down at the foot (think pendulum – again, this proved useful advice that I actually felt that I could implement).

- Have lack of mobility in ankles - ankle stretches before swimming (good advice and helped).

- Strong hamstrings creating the two-way pivot at the knee. All creating drag and holding you back.

- Toes kicking together 1-2-3, 1-2-3 – this confused me quite a bit. I had taught myself a two-beat kick by watching the Total Immersion DVDs and told Dan this. He said 1-2-3 1-2-3. He was definitely emphasizing shorter kicks, which would help a lot, but I was worried that I was going to tire my legs out for the bike and run. I'm not sure this was the best advice that I was given here, considering my ongoing left knee problem. I had no way of knowing what was aggravating my knee; whether it was running or swimming. It didn't seem to flare up on the bike though. If anything, when on the bike my other knee hurt a bit, as it was overcompensating for my left knee. Looking at Dan's website, he advocates kicking first and then moving onto other parts of the body. For me, at that time in my preparation, I feel it was definitely good advice, but a bit generic and not advice specifically tailored for me with my suspect left knee.

I say this because I had one lesson in October 2013 with Triathlon and now Ironman Pro Harry Wiltshire, who, just by observing my stroke and telling me how to move my arms better, managed to help me improve my 3km pool best time from 81 minutes to 68 minutes after one session. That is a significant improvement for just one lesson, and I was able to maintain that improvement and build on it week on week. If I had met Harry in April 2013, then there is no doubt in my mind that I would have gone quicker in Klagenfurt.

The fact is, of course, that I have to take the responsibility for my swimming, so that's just how it is, and I am sure Dan helps loads of people improve their swimming. He did help me improve mine and gave me more confidence, and I had a better swim time that I planned for Klagenfurt, but I felt I exhausted my legs out before it because of the drills. Harry's coaching had a much greater improvement on my swim performance than Dan's. I have to remember as well that without Nick showing me the ropes, I would still be lifting my head up and would do well to break 17 hours for an Ironman, as I'd be so tired from the swim, which I would have had to have done breast stroke, which would in turn have caused even more damage to my knee.

- Feet: turn the feet in, so they work together as a larger paddle

- Ankles: mobile and relaxed.... Frequent circling ahead of training.... Land based moves.... Yoga.... Dan recommended Bikram yoga. I tried it once in May, and it was fun and really hot. However, I went for an easy 40-minute run the same evening and nearly threw up. Again, I felt so tired from the training and did not want to overcook myself pre Klagenfurt.

- Knees: soft and not rigid. Not fixed on the all-important down sweep. A bend at the knee is essential on the downbeat of the kick, to send water backwards from the shin and the top of the foot.

- Hips: the kick originates in the gluteus and hip flexor region and only needs to be a small movement, 3-5cm at this point. By the time the small movement travels down the leg, it'll create the 30cm range that should be your maximum.

- Rotation: its fine for the legs to follow the rotation of the body - mobility to the trunk dictates that it'll be very hard for the legs to kick in a purely vertical plane anyway. But excessive movements and a lack of core control will lead to a splayed movement, so keep it small.

- Three or four shorter sessions each week is better than one long one, to learn new habits and unlearn bad ones.

- Dry land work each day....

- Stand on each leg, hold wall and pendulum foot.
  Turn ankles before swimming

- Drills:
  Holding steps under water, continuous kicking, let legs out slowly....
  Hold gluteus front crawl legs only. With the biomechanically correct straight kick leg up sweep, you'll feel the contraction of the muscle. Kick from knee and keep glutes soft. Release the hands up into a scull movement to come up for air, or use a central snorkel...

March 28th 2013

Swam 3km unaided and without breaks. 1hr 24mins. 2mins 48secs per 100metres 2008 strokes 33spl
24spm 58.78eff

Training runs 7.65 miles, 65mins
9.9 miles in 90 minutes – this was slower than I thought around Crystal Palace Park.

April 26th, end of hard week - ran 7.32 miles in 61mins, heart rate 165-170.
April 25th - swim 2 x 400 metres after drills. First 9mins 30sec. Second 10mins 0 sec

Sunday April 21st - My most pleasing training run of the year!!

Total distance covered - 17.04 miles. Total time - 2hrs 29mins. Long easy/medium intensity pace HR 165-170 (should become difficult only in the last 30 minutes); can do a few 30 second pick-ups to break up the slower pace, then back to the 165-170 HR. Pick it up the last mile to home.

I was really pleased with this run. The main thing was, I had no real aches at all, so that was good. My knee felt fine, so that was a relief. I'm pretty sure I would have carried three gels with me and would maybe even have run into a garage to get a bottle of water to drink and pour over my head around half way through. With just over 17 miles covered in just under 2 hours 30 minutes, I felt strong at the end and felt that a sub 4hr and definitely sub 4hr 30mins marathon was possible. I was holding back as well, although race day was to prove more of a test than I had envisaged, for more reasons than one.

Cycling Time Trials: the Novice

You need to join a cycling club to be able to compete in time trials, so I joined Dulwich Paragon. You can join most clubs for £20 for a year.

The three time trial races I'd scheduled on Nick's advice were three weekends in a row:

April 28th 2013 - TT Addiscombe 25 miles G25/53. Run 30-minute jog at IM pace after time trial
May 5th - TT Wigmore 25 miles Q25/8 – Race pace level 4 effort (Hr 185-190) starting at 170 for first 5 minutes then increasing. Run 45 minutes – after TT got for a 45-minute jog at IM pace.
May 12th – Bike 120 – TT Watford 50-mile TT – F1/50 Race pace level 4 again. Run 20 minutes after TT jog at IM pace.

April 28th 2013 - My first cycle time trial race 25 miles:

It was an early Sunday morning race, around an hour's drive from where I lived. I was really looking forward to my first 25-mile time trial race. I got there nice and early and was one of the first starters at 7.03 am. I parked up easily enough and went into the church hall to collect my number and pin it on. I was going to do a 30-minute run straight afterwards and felt super fit. After a few minutes of arriving, I noticed that everyone seemed to have a Cervelo bike and people were warming up on their turbos in the car park. I was not expecting to see that. Some of them even had a disc on their wheel. I had no idea how quick I could go and had no idea what a good position would be. Nick said that I would probably come last first time around but would go 10% quicker the following week, and not to worry, as none of the time trials were my A race. They were warms up to the big Ironman in Klagenfurt only two-and-a-bit months away.

It was fairly cold, so early on I thought I would wear my jacket. This was probably a mistake, as it was quite thick compared to what everyone else was wearing. I also had shorts on, compression socks and the fingerless gloves that I was used to.

The most complicated bit was finding where the start was. I asked a few other riders, and managed to work it out whilst following one of the race starters. The guy in front of me had a disc on his wheel and a Cervelo. There was someone holding his bike and giving him a push start. I was on one minute later. Everyone was spaced out one minute at a time. To enter the time trial was really good value for money; it only cost about £10. I had two bottles of water on my bike and an energy bar taped on my frame, which was way too much nutrition and added a bit of unnecessary weight. Nick had told me that it would be too much, but I thought that it would be better to have too much than not enough. I think that's quite common with inexperienced triathletes.

The guy in front was off, and I got ready. An old man with a clipboard checked my name and number. I told him it was my first ever time trial. Someone asked to hold my bike and give me a push start. I said, "No thanks," as it felt like cheating to me. 5, 4, 3, 2, 1. I had the bike in a hard gear and stood up and went for it. I was definitely slower starting than the guy in front. "Next time, I will get the push start," I said to myself.

The start was fairly flat, maybe even a little downhill. I heard it was a quick start and then there was a hill about five minutes in. I was just thinking, *I am going well here,* about five minutes in, when some guy just burned past me. The sight of his Cervelo and sound of his aero wheels and disc going past me sounded unlike any bike I had ever heard. It just sounded faster. I'd seen a few guys with zip wheels and aero bikes going past me out on the road, but not in race mode. It was an awesome and humbling site to behold. I thought that I would be like that in a few years, once I had built up my leg muscles. "It takes ten years to peak at this sport and I am still only nine months in," I told myself, "and anyway, this is not my A race. I have the endurance." I thought I would take a drink and try and stay close to him. He just went ahead into the distance, like I was on a scooter and he was on a motorbike, or a 50cc being overtaken by a 750cc.

I felt pretty good. I got 15 minutes into the race and nobody else had overtaken me. However, as a Marshall on a roundabout told me which way to turn, I noticed two or three guys nearby. The course was well laid out. Every now and then there was a sign with a black arrow and yellow background pointing where to go and another sign saying something like: "Cycling Race - Careful." There were cars on the road, but very few, as it was so early in the morning. The condition of the road was fairly good, although the course was a bit hillier than I thought. It was definitely not flat and not on a dual carriageway.

Another guy over took me at around 18 minutes, and then I held off the other two from behind. Then a miracle happened; I could see the guy in front of me with the disc on his wheel from the beginning - not the guy who burned past me: he was way too fast and was probably at home having a shower by now - no, the guy who had started in front of me.... I could see quite a slow uphill slope, but thought that I could take him ... I knew I could bide my time ... I was gradually gaining on him, and before I made my last push to leave him behind, I thought I would take a drink.... Big mistake. It was too steep ... I lost my balance and, as I came to a stop on my bike, rode into a ditch on the side of the road and did the world's slowest fall off my bike. I'd managed to pull my cleats out just in time and let go of my bike, so I had remained upright and was caught in a bank on the side of the road. It was like one of those videos that you send in to that ITV show presented by Jeremy Beadle, or a funny on YouTube. Annoyed, embarrassed and relieved, I picked the bike up, took the swig on my bottle that I had planned and a bit more and put it back in my cage. Then I got back on the bike and started again. I'd only lost about 15 seconds of time, but had learnt a big lesson…. I could not see the guy in front of me anymore, so I set about trying to find him again. I had been within 20 metres of him before I messed up, so I was motivated to go and make my first pass in a cycling time trial….

A few miles later I could see him again, and on a flat bit, the magical moment came. I went past him. My first overtake in a cycling time trial…. What a great feeling … a few minutes later, a couple of beasts with their zip wheels and aero bikes and aero helmets went past…. "They were not humans riding them anyway," I told myself, "and I will be super-human after a few more years of riding and training."

I was a bit slower than I thought I was going to be, but still riding faster than any of my rides on the road that I had done on my own. The race mind-set was more motivating, and of course there were no traffic lights on this course.

My Garmin was working pretty well, so I knew my heart rate, distance and time expired…. I pushed a bit towards the end and could see the chequered flag on the side of the road, with a couple of guys sat down recording the results. I'd come through unscathed, which was the most important thing, and it had taken me 1 hour 12 minutes. Not as good as I'd hoped, but I was safely through, and as I pedalled back in spinning mode, I got my bike back in, took a gel and got my running shoes on for my 30 minute run….

The run felt good…. I was glad to get off the bike all in one piece and took it easy on my run, following the heart rate exactly as Nick had laid out on my training plan….

When I got back to the village hall, they were writing all the times up on a board, and I was surprised how low down I had come. So many people had ridden it in under 1 hour and some of them had even gone 52 minutes. I stayed around to see the winners, mainly as inspiration. I also wanted to see their body shape, to see how lean I needed to be to compete with them. My time had given me a position way down the field, but not last. These time trial cyclists are really quick, but it was not my A race, Nick had said, and this was another small step to the big goal of completing Ironman Austria.

May 5th Wigmore 25 Mile - Time Trial Race 2

The following weekend and here I was; another early starter. This time, I was determined to go faster. I'd learnt a few things from the previous week. I got there nice and early. Another village hall or similar location, and I parked up to admire all the Cervelos, time trial bikes, aero helmets and people who could be bothered to get their turbos out in the car park so early in the morning and when it was so cold.

Time for the usual pre-race preparation. I had a look at the map where the start was and looked for a number starting that was lower than mine so I could follow them to the start line, as my sense of direction was awful. It was dry and I had pumped up my tyres the night before to 120. Probably too high, but I thought it would be less likely to give me a puncture. I decided to ditch the jacket, as I had got too hot the week before. I was pretty cold before the start, but figured that my body temperature would warm up soon enough once I got started. It was my fingers that were cold. I had my fingerless gloves on. In hindsight, I could have tried my thinner but not fingerless running gloves, although I didn't see anyone else doing that.

An added ingredient this time around was that my friend and neighbour Warren was doing the same race. I knew that he had an aero helmet and aero wheels and had gone under an hour, so figured if I could get near his time I would be improving. Nick had said I would go 10% quicker the following week, and I was determined not to fall off like a muppet this time around.

I got to the start, and the starter told me that officially I should not be allowed to race, but he would let me. I had my Orca 220-triathlon gear on. Tri shorts and a sleeveless top. He told me that, under British cycling rules, I should be wearing something covering my shoulders, in case I fell off, to avoid severe road rash. As I appreciated him letting me start, I blanked out what he said regarding falling. This time around I was on a mission. Yes, I would allow someone to give me a push start. Most people had long sleeve tops on and a lot of them had trousers on as well. I am a big guy, 6ft 3 ½, so I figured I would be warm enough once I got going, although I was shivering before the start a little bit….

So, this time … 10, 9, 8, 7, 6, 5, 4, 3, 2, 1…. With both wheels on my cleats, one of the starters was holding my bike and gave me a push off. Wow that must have saved me ... well, let's see ... I'm not sure, 2-3 seconds…. Who knows? Maybe it's a bit longer … I've got no idea, to be honest….

This time, it took much longer for someone to overtake me … around 15 minutes…. Of course, it all depends on what order people go out in…. I overheard a conversation in which someone said that they usually put the faster guys on near the end, as they know they can do under a certain time, so they can wrap the race up in good time…. They often put those of unknown speed at the start, as they are more likely to take a lot longer. Makes sense, I suppose….

This time, I felt like I judged my pace a bit better…. From what I remember, the course was well laid out again and the road surface was pretty good. It was fairly undulating, but there weren't too many turns…. I had no slip-ups falling off this time, which was a huge plus for my ego, of course…. I saw the time go by … 59 minutes … 1 hour … only a few miles to go … and really pushed the last bit…. I'd overtaken a few people along the way, and been overtaken by a few more than I'd overtaken, probably, as well. 1hr 1 ... 1hr 2 … 1hr 3 … 1hr 4…. Nearly there … 1hr 5 … can see the chequered flag…. I overtook a guy at the end who had overtaken me a mile or two back, although he had started a minute behind me, I think…. 25 miles in 1hr 6 minutes and 1 second. Yes I'd take that…. Over 10% quicker than the week before, finished safely and now I could go back to the car…. Have a drink of water and finish off my brick session with the run that Nick had laid out for me…. As I started out on my run, I saw a guy on his run, running in the opposite direction from his run, with a big grin on his face and an Ironman cap on…. He had a great running style and must have been quite a few years older…. He saw my Ironman visor, and gave a big smile ... I smiled back…. *That's it,* I thought…. *We are of the same mould … not just doing a time trial, but doing a brick session preparing for an Ironman.* I wondered how many Ironman races he had done…. More than me, that was for sure … as I had not done one yet and was still an Ironman virgin (a phrase I was to learn at the big race meeting in Klagenfurt a couple of months later….)

The run felt good. I was surprised how good my legs felt and also surprised at how fast I could run in the allowed heart rate. Not Craig Alexander style, but good for me at that time.... I saw Warren as I came back from my run....

"How did you do?" he asked.

"1 hour 5 or 6 minutes," I said, not knowing my exact time at that point. "How did you do?"

"1 hour 1 minute," he said.
"Well done," we both said.

I got some warmer gear on and went to the loo, then got some recovery food inside me; some carbs, water and energy drink. They were also selling cups of tea and fruitcake, so I had quite a bit of that. Warren and I had a good chat, as the race results came in ... I was quite pleased with my time. On a rating of 1-10 I was probably around 7 out of 10 with contentment. I was surprised how bad my position was still ... I mean, these time trial races are hard... Nick had said not to worry about the position, as a lot of the men and women who do it just focus on cycling, so you are usually coming up against cyclist specialists and not triathletes. However, there were quite a few triathletes there and a few Ironman athletes.

I knew the following week would be a bigger challenge, as it was a 50-mile time trial on a dual carriageway, with a short run to follow ... and I was only seven weeks out from Klagenfurt, when I was to do that race....

May 12th 2013 - 7 weeks from Klagenfurt – 3rd cycling time trial – 50-mile TT plus 20 minute run:

Here we are: my third cycling time trial and double the distance. The 50 miles was not even half the Ironman distance of the bike leg. Of course I had already done my crazy 111.7 bike ride to Brighton and back on the 7th April, so I knew I could do the full distance, but it had taken me forever and I'd stopped for a mackerel sandwich for 10 minutes and stopped for the toilet a couple of times and to get more water, but this speed rep would build my muscles and fine tune me a little bit more in seven weeks' time. I was following everything Nick said as best as I could and, as he was an Ironman veteran, felt in very good hands....

This time, I had another early start. I felt more confident going in and had some idea of what power I could go. I was not using a power meter. Mainly as it was yet another big expense, but also because I did not feel I had sufficient control of the bike to keep looking at a power meter. Also, deep down I probably did not want to push myself to the limit out on the road, and I had heard that 4-time Kona champion Chrissie Wellington had never used one, so neither would I.

I felt I could do the 50 miles in under 2hrs 20mins, if it went really well. That would mean 1hr 10mins per 25 miles. It should be a bit faster going on a dual carriageway and on a bit of a flatter course than the previous two. Also, it was my third time trial and I felt more comfortable on my bike. I'd got used to my aero bars during the winter on the turbo, so that was fine. It was just the question of how much power did I have in my legs and how much pain was I prepared to go through? Also, could I pedal round in a continuous motion and maximise the amount of energy I had? I had the two drinks bottles, and probably a couple of energy bars, which I would bite a piece off at a time every few minutes and then shove the rest under my shorts. This was a cool trick that Nick had showed me.

I remember feeling pretty good about the race, and I did not see many people during it; a few people went past me and I managed to overtake a few. More people went past me than I overtook, but they had the time trial bikes, aero wheels and aero helmets, and were going superfast. I had a nice felt road bike, which I'd got for £1,500, reduced from around £2200, with aero bars and no aero helmet or aero wheels. Also, my bicycle muscles were still in their first year, so I just did not have the power of some of the people who burnt past me. It was as simple as that.

I was really pleased with how my race was going, until around four miles from the end. I could see this guy in front of me with aero wheels and aero helmet. He was the guy who started 1 minute in front of me. I was about 10 seconds behind him, until we came to this big roundabout. He managed to go straight round it and I got caught up in traffic. Then he powered away. I lost sight of him at a crucial time. With three miles to go, I got to another roundabout that I had already crossed some 10-15 minutes before. I was meant to go straight on and the finish was three miles up the road. I saw a Marshall at the roundabout, and said:

"Which way do I go round here? I am exhausted."

He was on the opposite side of the roundabout that I was riding past. I rode around the other side, and he said:

"Go straight ahead...."

I was to find out later on that I was repeating part of the course. Ten seconds later, a beast of a bike-rider burnt past me.... It sounded like he said, "You are going the wrong way." I'm not sure if he said it or the Marshall said it; I know I was thinking it.... Over the next 10 minutes, several really fast bike riders overtook me.... Then I began to look at my watch every minute or two.... Oh no, I had gone past 50 miles and there was still no sight of the finish. All the numbers were a lot higher than me.... Then I saw a guy I had overtaken about half an hour before in front of me ... oh no....

I was angry, but kind of happy, as I knew it was even better for training. A few minutes later and I got to another roundabout ... I thought I had taken the wrong turning and was lost in another time trial race.... My main concern was that I was lost, and out of nutrition and drink, and had no money on me.... I got up to the roundabout and spoke to the Marshall. Everything kind of looked familiar....

I asked, "Is this the Watford TT 50 mile race?"

Low and behold, the guy who said yes was the same guy I had seen over 20 minutes before.

"You went the wrong way," he said, "I tried to tell you...."

I was wondering what he was talking about ... he confused me before ... still, I thanked him. He told me there was only 3 miles to go. I was so relieved that I was nearly finished.

I got on the bike and went up the road I should have gone up before.... When I got back I had a gel and some water, and did my short run to make it a brick session. They were putting the times up and I was embarrassed. Despite riding 60 miles, they had me up for the full time, so I was a lot quicker than it looked. I asked them to delete my time. I had beaten one or two people, but I think they were over 70, maybe even 75 years of age.... That is one of the inspirational things about Ironman. Some people just keep going, no matter how old they are. I'd love to be super-fit when I am in my 70s or 80s, or even 120s - who knows what's possible? Dream on, Jase....

Here were my splits ... according to the fact that I was less than 1 minute behind the guy who started in front of me. He had a time of 2 minutes 16 seconds at 50 miles, so that was my time as well.

Then, as I remember from my Garmin, my other time was 56 miles (half Ironman distance), 2 hours 31 minutes; 60 miles, 2 hours 41 minutes. *Not a bad training session,* I thought. As the minutes went by and I started talking to people, I found it funnier and funnier, and they had some great cakes and a nice cup of tea in the church hall to get the carbs in.... *What an experience all that was,* I thought.

I had some other big bike days planned before Klagenfurt. A few of the notable ones were on May 19th 240 bike – HR 140-160, June 4th 180 bike – HR 150-170, June 9th 240-300 bike – the rest can be seen on my complete training guide at the end of the book...

I was recording my training every day as I started out. However, as the training increased, I was busier texting it to Nick, as well as recovering, refuelling and writing down strategy notes for the Ironman Klagenfurt, which was soon to be on the horizon. Before that, there was a little Half Ironman test in the first week of June to warm me up.

June 2nd 2013 – Half Iron Triathlon – North Fambridge

This was a big day for me. My first Half Iron distance, and only four weeks away from Klagenfurt. Well, very nearly a half distance. It was a 1.9km swim in open water with a current, so that bit was actually a bit harder, and the full 90km bike on an undulating course. You actually had to stop in two places, as it was too dangerous to just carry on riding onto the crossroads. That must lose me 30 seconds, right, and then the run was slightly shorter, at 18km instead of 21km. So a half Ironman distance, apart from the 3km running at the end. It was not an official Half Ironman event, so had to call itself something different, hence the name Half Iron.

Here is a summary of the race set-up and course.

The bike racking took place on race morning from 6:30am. All athletes need to be at the swim start by 7:55am for the race briefing. T Shirt and a goody bag.

Deep-water start in the tidal River Crouch. Wharf and pontoon provide perfect spots for spectators. Athletes will start at 8:10am and complete 2 loops of the course. Water safety marshals will be present with motorised boats and canoes. Please note this is a tidal river and will be more challenging than a typical open water or pool swim. Wetsuits are compulsory. Swim cut-off strictly 9:20am.

The cycle course takes athletes out of North Fambridge and onto the quiet scenic roads of the Dengie Peninsula. Here you will pass through small towns and villages with traditional weatherboard homes, negotiate the Burnham Bends and experience a fast and flat course over the marshes. Athletes will complete 2 laps of the course.

The run course is situated around North Fambridge Village. Here spectators will have plenty of opportunity to enjoy the triathlon. Huge crowds of spectators line the run course and provide plenty of support for the athletes. Athletes will start the run by heading out along the sea wall before turning inland to run through the village. Here you will see your fellow triathletes on the last part of the cycle. The run will then take athletes through open fields and past the aid station before returning to the transition and finish area. Surface is a mixture of paved roads, paths, trail, grass and gravel. Please be careful and always listen to marshals instructions... they have given up their time for your benefit.

I went to bed the night before the race at around 8.00pm. In the morning, I left the house around 4.30am. I had my by now customary strong coffee on waking and made a coffee flask for when I arrived at the venue. I allowed 1 hour 30 minutes to get there by car, and needed it, as I took a wrong turning or two in the dark, looking at the sat nav incorrectly as the coffee was waking me up. Noticing one of the Marshalls just off the main road, I parked up in a field and saw that I was one of the first to arrive. I decided to walk down to the transition area and take a look at the set-up and the river. I knew I had the fitness to complete the race but I was very nervous about my first open water swim. I'd swum in the ocean before on holiday of course, but only a few hundred metres away from the shore, and if I had been swimming for a long time I would have had a boogie board with me. That was when I was 19 years old.

Now, at the ripe old age of 38, I was doing my first Half Iron race.... That was a cool feeling ...it made me feel like half a person if I could finish this race ...yes, half of an Ironman!! So, kind of half-superhuman. One of the reasons I decided to do the Ironman was because it was the hardest thing I could think of possibly doing, so therefore I thought if I could cope with the daily discipline and pressures needed to do that, then I felt I could be a better parent, a better partner, run my business better and help more people in life.... For me, the Ironman was a symbol of wanting to be better at everything in my life, and every other aspect of my life had improved along with it. Having Nick as a coach was a driving force, not only for my training but the discipline in Ironman became a metaphor for the rest of my life. The more you put into life, the more you get out of it. I remember reading Arnold Schwarzenegger's autobiography once, and he said he would rather live life than be a spectator of it. That's exactly how I felt about Ironman and Half Irons.

As I walked down to the transition, I felt pretty good. I was probably the first person to go the loo cubicle, which was good, as it still smelt nice and there was no queue. I saw that all the numbers in transition had a specific place. I picked up my goodie bag and a T-Shirt, and got some help putting my race belt on, as this was the first time I had used a race belt. I was getting more into this racing lark. I planned to get in the top half of the field.

I walked over to the river and saw the current. It looked pretty strong and quite daunting. I'd tried putting my wetsuit on a couple of times at home and had used it once at the Brockwell Lido with Nick, where it was so cold that we did not stay in for too long. Looking at the current, I saw the buoys and it looked like a long way. There were a couple of other guys there. I asked one guy what he thought and if he had done any races before. He said he had done dozens of Half Ironmans and half a dozen full Ironmans. He said the current was quite strong and easy going out, but hard coming back, and that you'd want to get out quickly or you could get tired. *Great,* I thought. I knew I was going to be towards the back of the pack at the swim… but I could then start to overtake people on the bike….

I'd parked my car a good five minutes from the transition area, so walked quickly back and got my bike in transition…. It's amazing how quickly time goes by on race morning…. One minute I was the first athlete there, and then, what seemed like only a few minutes later, transition was packed and I was putting my wetsuit on in the cold…. I got talking to the guy next to me, who said he had done the race last year and that it was a nice course. He said he was a rubbish swimmer, so I thought there was no way I was drafting him.

I put the wetsuit on, which took me ages. Easily 5, probably 10 minutes. I made sure I put enough body glide on, although it would turn out I did not put enough on the neck of the suit, as I was to have a bruise in the evening. I'd like to say it slowed down my swim time before I reveal it to you, but I don't think it really did. I could feel it a little bit during the race but not much.

It was a buoy start. The race was organised really well and everyone was called forward for a briefing 10 minutes or so before the start. I moved near the front. I decided I wanted to try and draft some faster swimmers, although I had not ever been able to do that in the swimming pool, as the good swimmers were way too quick for me and the rubbish ones would slow me down and get in the way.

We walked in … the first few seconds felt freezing, as the temperature was 15 degrees, but it soon felt warm enough. I was the only person that I could see with a special Blueseventy hood on. Nick had suggested it, and I think that was a good move. It did go round my neck and make me look a bit of a wally, but this was a small price to pay. I felt really nervous at the swim start. There were so many people…. I was at the front at the start and they said "2 minutes, 1 minutes to go…." Treading water, I got squeezed up against the starting buoy…. The guy on the microphone shouted for everyone to come back…. It got more and more crowded and my heart rate increased … then the countdown … 10, 9, 8 … 5, 4, 3, 2 … quick, start Garmin 910 on race mode … 1 … 0….

Go…. I was in the first or second row. I decided I would have a quick start and draft…. I put my head underwater and could not see anything at all, apart from mud and some really weird what looked like tadpoles. So much for drafting…. In the first minute and a half, I swam into about 10 people from behind and the side … each time, it would stop my stroke and I would look up…. A couple of minutes in, it thinned out and I started to enjoy it…. The first part was down stream…. The wetsuit was keeping me buoyant…. I started breathing every four strokes, but soon realised I was going way off course…. It started to thin out and I was getting further behind the leaders … people would still overtake me, but less and less people…. I discovered that my sighting was rubbish. I had watched quite a few sighting videos on YouTube, and had the Total Immersion open water DVD that shows it, but had not practiced it much in the pool. Each time I did it, I almost came to a complete stop, got a mouthful of muddy water, or could feel my neck rubbing against my wetsuit, or all three…. So I sighted less and less and went on instinct. I would swim for 30 seconds without looking, and then look up and realise I had gone way too far left or way too far right…. The swim was two loops of the course … during that time, I was told I was off course at least five times by people in canoes. One time I swam into a boat. There were lots of boats in the middle. I was used to breathing to the right hand side and for this course I needed to look left the whole time. I wished I had done more bi-lateral breathing drills, as Nick had suggested in the training … I had done half of them, but did not feel as confident breathing left. Halfway through the swim, I was breathing left as well, as I thought that was a quicker way to finish…. I went through each buoy doing breaststroke, as I could not see anything out of my goggles. They were tight enough, so that was fine, but it was cloudy through them. A trick I learnt later from Nick was to spit inside the goggles before using them every time, and this works wonders, believe me. I do it every race and every time I go to the pool nowadays.

Anyway, back to the race…. One time I saw 30 people or so in front and decided I would catch them up … I really went for it and looked up again. They had gone further ahead, but that's because I had gone too far right. It seemed like I had just gone sideways and had to swim twice as long to just get back to where I was…. I know the distance can be deceiving, and I probably did not go as far left or right as I thought, but I think I would have come first if there was a prize for swimming the least straight. The main thing was that I felt good. Halfway through the second lap, I really started to relax and enjoy it…. Part 1 of 3 was nearly completed…. I swam into one guy about five times in 3 minutes and apologised and said I would buy him a beer afterwards. He laughed and told me not to worry about it…. Then I got to the last buoy, and a guy in a boat said:

"You've done it, nearly there…."

I was about 100 metres from the exit and went for my à la Michael Phelps finish…. This consisted of one of the world's ugliest triathlon swimming finishes, no doubt…. As I got to the last 10 metres I could see a small crowd of people cheering, and some volunteers even helped me out of the water. *This is like Hawaii Ironman,* I thought to myself. I was trying to undo the back of my wetsuit and struggling, when another competitor did it for me without asking, and I offered to do the same for them. Not sure if that was allowed or not, but very sporting nonetheless….

I looked at my swim watch … just over 50 minutes … wow…. Best I had hoped to swim at would have been around 45 minutes, so 50 minutes was not too bad…. Now, transition, and onto my strength, the bike…. The weakest of my three disciplines, the swim, was over. I jogged up at a reasonable pace to the transition area. I was pretty cold coming out and felt my right calf jolt and then release. I had had that once or twice before in the pool, so thought it would be OK once it released itself. I just thought I would start on a slightly easier gear on the bike and keep my cadence up instead.

When I got to the transition area, I realised that almost all of the bikes had already gone. Not good. However, I still had a great feeling of achievement, having completed my first open water swim. I dried my feet with a towel, faffed around a bit, put on my jacket and manually put my shoes on, as I did not have the confidence to get on my bike and put my shoes on as I rode.

Then, away onto the bike … I took a few swigs of my energy drink and away I went … overtaking people straight away. I could not believe how slow some people were going. I guess they were good swimmers and I wasn't. I knew I was pretty fit. I was surprised how some people were quite a bit overweight. I'd slimmed down quite a lot and changed body shape.... I was looking more skinny than lean, probably, but was pleased to overtake some people.... Three or four minutes in, and I thought I would take the first bite of my first power bar.... I undid it from my frame, took a bit and nicely slipped the bar under my shorts. Nick said it was good to bite a bit at a time every 20 minutes, so my stomach did not get too full.... I felt great on the bike … overtaking one person at a time, and then, if I saw a group of people, I would gauge the distance and have a big swig of my lemon isotonic (the same one that was going to be at the aid stations in Klagenfurt) and proceed to overtake more than one, the whole group, or drop in somewhere in between, so the person I had just overtaken had to move back.... One thing for sure, it was hard to get into a rhythm. The course was definitely not flat … road surfaces were good, and there weren't many cars around at the start, as it was still early morning, but the course went up and down like a yo yo. At times, it felt like riding around Crystal Palace where I lived....

At the end of the first leg of my bike, I had caned both of my isotonic drinks and knew I would need to stop to go to the toilet. There was one guy on the bike who I was racing against, almost … I saw him come by me and vice versa a couple of times … I'd seen him go to the loo and pushed hard for a bit.... Then I saw someone else taking a leak by a farm gate and decided to do the same. It was the longest pee I'd ever had. It seemed to last for about four minutes and got rid of the slight stomach ache I had.... As I was peeing, I could see a guy in a field walking from a few hundred metres away; he was only about ten metres away by the time I bolted. I was worried that he was a Marshall who was going to disqualify me, but I did not stop to hang around....

I resumed with renewed energy. I could then see the guy I'd been racing against in front of me.... Then, from another road came three blokes, who were definitely in the same race … they were going really slowly and laughing a lot.…

"I hope we don't get caught," one of them said.

It looked like they had cheated … I mean, why else would they have had race numbers on and said that. I burnt past them and caught the guy up who I'd been racing against.… I burnt as fast as I could down a nice downhill section, and 3-4 minutes later he pulled alongside me and said:

"I thought you lost me miles back."

"I went for a pee," I said. He said the same … he said he was exhausted. I said we were doing well, as we had overtaken about 30-40 people on the bike by that point.… I then tried to burn ahead on a flat part, as I was worried we were going to get done for drafting. I find that, as a big guy, I tend to be better on the flat parts and not so great going uphill. I am not that great on steep downhill slopes, as I am still getting used to controlling the bike at top speeds … so much to learn in Ironman, hey? It's like anything else I suppose; if you want to be good at something, you have to put the effort in.…

Five miles from the finish of the bike leg … just going well and there was a traffic jam and a bloody tractor in front of me … ahhhhghghghhghhghgh … there were two cars in front … I tried to overtake and nearly got run over.… Forget that.… Let's stay in one piece, shall we? This is a B race, not my A race.… Five minutes later, there were a group of five or six riders that had caught up, all thinking of doing the same.

"Don't overtake," I said. The road was narrow and uphill, and there were cars zooming past in the opposite direction. Then, with two to three miles to go, the tractor turned off.

I was estimating that it cost me around two minutes (it had probably cost me more like thirty seconds), but was saving my legs for the run, which was good.

So the tractor was out of the way, and I thought I would really push the last couple of miles. All the way round, I was surprised how slow my bike time was. 2hrs 54 minutes. I felt good. It was just that the course was a lot hillier than the time trials and my legs were probably pedalling in one gear lower than on the time trials, as the power just wasn't there after the swim and I wanted to pace myself for the run afterwards. Bottom line is, I just did not have the strength I wanted in my legs to keep the pedals at a high enough speed in a hard enough gear. The stronger your legs, the harder you can go. I felt my endurance was pretty good.

So, to T2. From my recollection, that bit remains a bit of a blur. I do remember I had put P20 on for the first time pre-race, as the weather forecast was for sun. It had been raining a bit during the swim but had started to clear up during the bike ride. Obviously, I must have put my bike back in transition and put my run shoes on.
I had been bursting to go to the loo again for a few minutes, and took my opportunity as soon as I'd run away from the crowd. There was quite a big healthy crowd coming into T2. A couple of hundred people. This made it even more of a buzz coming in. As I ran past onto the run course, they even said my name and how I was running for the Chipmunka Foundation (see www.chipmunkafoundation.org), to save lives for people with mental illness. That was awesome. They also said how I was training for Ironman Austria, which felt great.

I stopped my bike time and started my run time. My automatic triathlon racing program I had set up on my Garmin had gone wrong, as I had pressed the wrong button, but I had the split times of the swim, bike course and now run working. It was just the transitions that I had not put on my watch, and the timing of each event was a few seconds out, as I was a bit disorganised.

We had to run four 4.5km laps. It was a mix of concrete and off road grass and also included running over a train track ... I hoped I was going to miss the train and run straight through.

So, 90 seconds into the run I saw my opportunity. I had held my position until then. I decided to go to the toilet for the last time during the race. I went away from the crowd and Marshalls and just peed off the running course. I'd seen someone in front do the same, so figured it was a good place to do it. I had no idea if I was allowed to go there or not, but if you have to go then nature calls, right? I lost three or four positions at least, as I was removing another two bottles of water that I had refilled at the start of the second leg on the bike course. I can remember stopping on the bike course and getting a volunteer/Marshall to help me fill up my water bottles. It was a good move, as it started to get hot later on during the bike and by the time the run started it was super warm.

So once I had finished my pit stop, I decided to try to not allow anyone overtake me unless they had a different wristband on. At the end of each lap you were given a different coloured wristband. So for the first lap you didn't have one, once you finished lap one you received your first wristband, once you finished lap two you received your second wristband, once you finished lap three you received your third and final wristband and then once you were finishing lap four you went straight ahead to the finishing shoot instead of turning left to carry on and do another lap.

I was running at a specific heart rate very slightly higher than Ironman pace. That was around 170-175 heart rate. I felt pretty good on the run. My legs were not as stiff as I thought they would be. I maintained a 9-minute mile pace at my heart rate. If I was below a 9-minute mile nearing the end of a mile, I would put a bit of a surge in for 50-100 metres and make sure I got under 9 minutes, before letting my heart rate go back down again.

This was not what Nick had told me to do, but I was thinking of holding my position, and it also seemed important psychologically to go under 9 minutes for each mile.

The run started off with a lovely run along the riverbank with the crowd, then onto a big field, out onto a main road and into a trail run. There were a couple of gates to go through, which slowed you down a bit. The odd runner went past me on the first lap, but anyone who did already had a wristband or two, so it did not worsen my overall position. I overtook a few people as well, which was confidence-boosting. I thought that they must have been good swimmers and fairly good on the bike, as I thought I had done quite well on the bike and my swim was pretty poor.

There were a few farm gates, then you had to slow down and stop and walk through then the train track, with a Marshall stood there. Fortunately, first time around it was all clear and I could run straight through.

Coming onto the end of the first lap, someone gave me a wristband. *This is cool,* I thought. *One of the four laps completed and then I am a Half Iron Person.* Then I carried on running straight ahead.… I then saw this guy with a big belly racing past me at what seemed like twice my speed. The commentator said:

"It's a race for seventh place.…"

I realised that I had run up the finishing shoot instead of turning left onto lap two. I got about five metres from the finish and then smiled, saying that I'd gone the wrong way. I saw the other guy finish.... I thought it was hilarious. I'd lost about 10-15 seconds running the wrong way, but it gave me a bit of an adrenaline rush and I could not stop laughing. Then I was coming out onto lap two and they said my name again on the microphone:

"This is Jason Pegler. He is raising money for the Chipmunka Foundation and training for Ironman Austria." It gave me another lease of life for lap two.

The second lap was a little more difficult. My average heart rate was a bit harder and I was breathing a little heavier. There were a couple of aid stations on each lap. I was drinking a small glass of water at each and then pouring a bit over my head … slowing down and bending forward, making sure I did not throw it all over my socks and get my feet wet and risk potential blisters, which would not be a cunning plan.

There were less people overtaking, as the best athletes had finished. I was overtaking more people, as some people were getting tired, and it was great to see people either coming up or that I was overtaking with no wristband on yet. That meant that I would beat all of them, as long as I kept running.

Second time around I had got through the train track again without having to watch a train go past. Phew. I noticed that I was still going under 9-minute miles, but had to put in a little longer surge at about 0.90 of a mile to make sure I got under 9 minutes. My Garmin was working fine, so that was a good sign for Klagenfurt when I would really need it, or so I thought. OK, lap two was finished and I was given another coloured armband that I put on my wrist.

I told myself that there were just two more laps to go. I was feeling pretty tired, but was fit enough to sense that I could run the whole run course. In my head, I was trying to go under 5 hours and 30 minutes. Before the start of the race I had hoped to go under 5 hours, but my bike leg was 30 minutes slower than I thought it was going to be. It was just much hillier than I thought it would be.

Anyway, I was very satisfied that my running legs felt good. They still felt relatively light - lighter than they had in Chilham and in the BallBuster, and this was a longer race. I was a few months further on in my training and development as an athlete, so this was not surprising. My coach had trained me well.

Lap three. I drank less water, as I did not feel like it, and poured more over my head. I had an Ironman visor on so that I would feel the cold water on my head. I know it's cheesy, as I had not even done an Ironman yet, but for me it was a positive anchor wearing it, as it made me feel like I could do a Half Iron race easier.

Lap three was going fine. The course was thinning out by now, as more people had finished, but I could see people with one band or no bands and that really spurred me on. This time, if I saw people walking it spurred me on. A few times I would run past and say, "Come on mate, keep going," and people would say, "Thanks". I must admit that one or two people who were on my lap did go past me, but only a couple. I had thought that I would not allow that on the last lap, but had better keep to my approximate heart rate for now.

I was given my third armband, and the guy who gave it to me said:

"Come on, just one lap to go."

The end of each lap was inspiring, as you could see and hear the finishing chute, got given the armband and then had the crowd cheering you on. This is when it got really mentally tough. My heart rate was going up and my pace was slowing.… I was having to put longer surges in to go under 9 minutes a mile and just about did that OK.…

On the final lap I saw hardly anyone at all with three wristbands on, just a couple who I overtook. There were plenty of people with one or two on and a few with none yet. *Poor people,* I thought. It was getting really hot now and the sun was blazing down. I was really pleased I had put on the P20 sun cream before the race.

I was really doing well … proud of myself … I was running within myself and maintaining my position. The race was really spaced out by now. Then, with about 0.20 miles to go on my Garmin, I saw this girl coming up quickly. *Blimey, she is fast,* I thought, and she was compared to me (her run split turned out to be under 1hrs 30 minutes). She came up alongside me and I saw it. *Oh no, she has 3 wristbands on as well,* I thought. *There is no way I am letting anyone overtake me. I have been saving my energy for this.* I started swinging my arms, probably like an ape and not an Olympic marathon runner, and raced to stay ahead. She kept coming.…

This continued until we were only a few hundred metres from the finish. She just got level with me, and I saw her look left where the guys giving the bands are ... I thought to myself, *No way - she is going to go the wrong way....* I already knew exactly where the finishing chute was, and you were slightly blind to it as you came in ... so I thought I would let her go ahead.... She did exactly that. She went the wrong way, until one of the guys giving the bands out told her. As she had gone left, she had to stop her stride and turn around. I was 1 metre behind her then ... by the time she turned around, I was 5 metres ahead.... There were 100 metres to go and I ran as fast as I could ... I'd beaten her by 3 seconds. Bit cheeky I know, but it's amazing what people can find in their legs at the end of a race....

At the end I was given a medal straight away, which was placed on my neck. There were people saying well done. There was a drinks table, where I had a few small drinks and took some energy bars, and even some cake, I think. I'd done it. I was a Half Iron athlete. *Blimey, Klagenfurt is going to be hard,* I thought, *but I can do it ... I can do it ... I just did this ... yes!*

My overall time was 5 hours 33 minutes and 3 seconds. My final position was 90th out of 167 finishers. I was fairly pleased with the time, but it would have been nice to go under 5 hours 30 minutes. I did feel a bit frustrated that I had not come in the top half of the field. "Oh well, next time I'm sure I will," I told myself.

After the race I made sure I walked around a bit, as I had read somewhere that this was a good thing to do so you did not get too stiff. I filled up with carbs and protein and rehydrated. It was a job well done. Then I set about driving back. I was extremely pleased when I got home. I tried the medal out on my little boy Oscar, who was five at the time, and my daughter Anna, who was two. They both liked it. Now I had a medal for Chilham, a BallBuster hoodie, a Cranleigh 21 mile medal and a Half Iron North Fambridge Medal. Next up was the big one: a full Ironman medal. The ultimate challenge.

Full breakdown of North Fambridge Splits:

Swim time: 50.33 Split position 148
T1 3.35
Bike: 2:54:39 Split position 64
T2 1:37
Run: 01:42:36 Split position 85

I had a lovely bath and ate loads for the rest of the day. I also had a really deep sleep that night, probably swimming into more boats during my dreams. I had done the perfect warm up to Klagenfurt, or so I thought until the next day.

Post Fambridge Race

I felt good the afternoon and evening after North Fambridge. However, the next morning things were not quite right. I woke around 6am with a massive headache. At first I thought I was just exhausted from the day before, but then I went straight to the bathroom and threw up big time. Oh no. Then I just felt worse. I ended up spending most of the day in bed. I tried to eat, but just couldn't keep anything down. There was a 24-hour sickness bug going around at the time, and indeed, within a week, my son and daughter were both poorly. I spoke to Nick about it, and he said that I may have picked something up from the river. I think that is most likely. Whatever the cause, I was absolutely shot to pieces. It was the worst I had felt for a long time.

I ended up missing three days training on my hardest week.
They were big sessions… The day after Fambridge, Monday the 3rd of June, I was meant to do 60 minutes of swim drills and 60 minutes revs and recovery on the turbo. Then, on Tuesday the 4th of June, I was meant to do a 3 hour bike ride at 150-170 heart rate and on Wednesday the 5th of June, I was meant to do a 100 minute mega run fast repetitions session – described as a breakthrough workout by Nick. This consisted of six laps of Crystal Palace Park, alternating between (HR 150-160) on one lap and (HR 180-190) on the next.

Fambridge had given me confidence, but missing the three days could have been crucial in my predicted time for Klagenfurt. I would never have any way of knowing, and would just have to do the best I could.

By Thursday the 6th of June, I felt OK and made sure that I hit every session after that. I did not feel as strong as normal for a few days, but managed to complete each session.

Tapering Weeks, Hooray!

I had three weeks of tapering before my A race, Klagenfurt.
Taper week one: only 6 hours, Taper week two: only 4 - 4.30 hours and Taper week three - race week - only 2 hours.

During the taper, I definitely enjoyed the free time that came with less training. I also felt happy, as I knew I had done all the hard work. My body also started to feel stronger as I became less fatigued. My fitness was still high and my energy levels were increasing. I took it as easy I could and spent some more time with my family and working. Details of my tapering are below. I managed to do every session, although on race week I eased off a bit more than suggested, and I'll explain why in the Klagenfurt chapter coming later on....

10th June: Bike 40mins – revs and recovery 10mins at 95 rpm on +1 gradient, increase 5rpm every 5mins up to 115 and finish with 10mins on 95rpm on gradient.

11th June: Swim 45mins drills/glide WU, 15 x 50-metre reps going fast, leaving every 90 seconds. 5-min WD with lots of kick with float drills.

12th June: 40mins – 10-min WU, 3 laps of CP park loop, half lap fast (uphill to top and down to sharp left turn before fence) – half easy (downhill bit past pond/auditorium).

13th June: Swim long – 100mins – Over distance (Ironman) swim 4km – wear Garmin 910 and note pacing

14th June: Rest

15th June: Rest

16th June: Bike 90mins – Tatsfield Loop, HR 160-180, spinning small ring with some pushes on hills and big ring intervals of 2-5mins – I did Biggin Hill instead, as know that route better.

Week starting 17th June – Taper week 2 – only 4-4.30 hours

17th June: Bike 40mins – Revs and recovery 10mins at 95rpm on +1 gradient, increase 5rpm every 5mins up to 115 and finish with 10mins at 95rpm on) gradient.

18th June: Swim 30mins – to pool and 30 lengths every other one fast (above race pace)

18th June: Bike 30mins power intervals 5mins WU – 20 x 30 seconds at 400 watts with 30 secs recv at 150 watts, 5 WD at 95 rev 190 watts.

19th June: Run 30mins – 10-min WU, 3 laps of CP park loop, half lap fast (from top of hill along straight, round sharp left turn to next right, down the hill by lake/pond/auditorium) then slow down round bottom corner and uphill, easy, easy, easy until fast again at a line from the top.

20th June: Swim – Long reps – 5-min drills, then main set fast 200 metre reps in under 4mins x 4, then 5mins kick set

21st June: Bike 35mins – Sweetspot/Threshold intervals 1 x 20mins. WU 5mins bring cadence up to 95 and power up to 200w on gradient +1, 2 x 10 minutes at power 260 on gradient +2, 5mins

easy at gradient 0 (power 150-180), then repeat 20 minutes at power 260 on gradient +2, WD for 5mins at 95rpm Power 190.
22nd June: Rest
23rd June: Bike 60 minutes – HR 160-180 spinning small ring. All small ring.

Week starting 23rd June – race week Taper 3 – only 2 hours

24th June: Rest
25th June: Run 20-30mins – 10-min WU to run route , 5 x 'pick-ups'/strides… bouncing along … fast controlled, for 200 metre efforts at 8 out of 10 effort level (HR won't have time to respond quickly enough). WD 5-10 minutes easy.
25th June: Bike 40-45mins – on turbo 10mins warm up, to include 4 x 2 minute hard efforts at 95rpm cadence; gradient +2; at 300-340 watts, with 2 minutes recovery at 100-150 watts in between efforts, 10mins warm down.
25th June: Run 20-30mins – 10-min WU to run route, 5 x 'pick-ups'/strides… bouncing along … fast controlled, for 200 metre efforts at 8 out of 10 effort level (HR won't have time to respond quick enough). WD 5-10 minutes easy.
26th June: Swim 20mins – to pool and 20 lengths, every other one fast (above race pace)
27th June: Run 30mins – walk/run after your journey will feel dulled by travel - just easy jog or even some walking. Do 3 x 100 metre bursts/strides (with 2mins easy between) to kick start metabolism near the end.
27th June: Lots of hydration, take junior aspirin before flight and wear compression socks.
28th June: When bike is assembled take it for a test spin, 20-25 minutes down the side of the lake and back
Total rest - can get some sunshine and swimming on the pier to prepare for race day.
29th June: 15-min swim, 15-min bike and 10-min jog in race kit
STAY OUT OF SUN AND HYDRATE (with Dioralyte) ALL DAY
30th June: Ironman Austria – Race Day!!

Klagenfurt Ironman Race!! Can he do it??

I travelled to Austria on Thursday the 27th of June. The race was on Sunday the 30th June at 7.00am.

Thursday 27th of June

Nick drove me to the airport with my bike, which was great. I asked him for any last minute tips, and he gave me some great advice. He also bought me a Triathlon book written by Johnny and Alistair Brownlee, which was a nice touch. He wished me luck and drove off. There I was at the airport, an Ironman in waiting. I checked my bags in, which were totally full of Ironman gear. I could not fit my massive pump in, as it did not fit in my suitcase.

I then put my bike in. Nick had lent me a bag to put my bike in. Then I saw some other people sat down at the side of the airport room. They looked like me. They had Ironman merchandise on and were clearly on their way to Klagenfurt for the race. There were about half a dozen Ironman athletes, with three or four additional partners/family members. I got talking to a couple that shared the same kind of excitement and anticipation for the big day ahead. One or two more Ironman athletes arrived with some serious bike boxes, and I told them where to put their bikes. It felt great to meet so many like-minded people.

When I got on the aeroplane, I sat next to an Ironman athlete. He was a nice guy and he said that it was his fifth Ironman race. I asked him a few questions about Klagenfurt, and he had raced it twice. He was definitely a few kilos overweight, so it just goes to show that you don't have to have the perfect body to complete an Ironman, although it would help you go quicker the better body you have, no doubt about that.

I spoke more to the other guy next to me, a young guy who was intrigued about the whole Ironman race and the considerable long distance. When the Ironman guy heard me talking about my predicted times to the other guy, he interrupted, saying there was no way I would be able to run off the bike. I just thought, *I'll focus on the positives and I've done the training.*

As we landed, we collected our kit, and by the time we were all at Nirvana Europe there must have been about 50 of us; 35 Ironman athletes with about 15 partners/family members. We flew to Slovenia first and then drove to Klagenfurt on a coach. The landscape that we drove through was beautiful, and the coach journey took around 90 minutes. It was great, as they had the previous year's Ironman Klagenfurt race on the television; the race where the English man Phil Graves stormed into the lead onto the bike and led out of T2, but soon got overtaken and ended up pulling out, having gone too hard and cooking up in the extraordinary heat.

I spent most of the trip speaking to a policeman who was racing his second Ironman. He had done Frankfurt the year before in 13 hours and was now aiming for the same time as me; under 12 hours. We were having a great chat until he got off at an earlier hotel and I wished him good luck for the race. Then we pulled up to my hotel.

I was staying at the Seepark Hotel, the official Ironman Klagenfurt race hotel. Nick had advised that I stay somewhere quieter, so that I could stay out of all of the excitement. I understood what he was saying, and was definitely going to take his advice on not doing the bike tour in a mini bus the day before and staying well away from the expo until after the race, as I thought that would, like Nick said, wear me out.

However, I had not bought my entry fee directly from Ironman, but had paid Nirvana Europe directly for my entry. Of the hotels they had available, the Seepark Hotel was the best and also the nearest to the swim start. I figured that I could get the best of both worlds by taking this option, and I had to book my accommodation with Nirvana if I wanted to get my entry ticket from them, as Ironman had sold out on their website.

When I arrived at the hotel, I was very pleased. It was a beautiful hotel, and I had a massive room, easily enough space for my bike and to lay all my kit out and also have enough space to switch off from it. There was only a shower though, unfortunately, which was not ideal. Apart from that, it was great. There was also a nice view of the canal from my window.

I checked in all my gear and unpacked everything. Good - I felt nice and organised. Then I found out where the bike fitters were from Nirvana and checked when they were fitting my bike together. They said there was a bit of a delay, but they would have it done later that night so I could use it the following morning. *Fine with me,* I thought. I rehydrated from the plane and decided I would do as Nick said and go for an easy run. What was meant to be a short run and then back to the hotel turned into me thinking, *I'll do a little run and then register and get it out of the way.*

I ran out of the hotel to the park and asked a few people where registration was. It was pretty easy to find the Ironman expo but the registration was harder. There were athletes everywhere warming up and walking about, mixed in with the locals going around their everyday business. There were also a lot of volunteers helping out. I ran up to the finishing line and could see it from side on. It was great to see the temporary stadium they had built. I found the expo overwhelming, so cut my run a bit short and thought, *I'll register and then go and chill out back in the room before dinner.*

Eventually, I found the register. I was meant to pay six euros for something, I forget what, but I did not have any money with me, so they waived it. It may have been for a day race licence. This led to me having to go down to registration a couple of days later, but they said they would let me off paying it then. Anyway, with registration I got my goodie bag. I had a free rucksack, a swimming hat that said Ironman on it, a few flyers and a programme with the schedule on it, etc.... I think I was also given my time chip that I would have to wear in the race, although they may have given me that when I dropped my bike off the day before the race....

Anyway, registration completed, I jogged back to the hotel slowly, as I had cut my run short. I went back to the room and had some water, and then it was time for dinner. I went downstairs and had a really healthy meal. Salad, carbs, protein ... a bit of everything and some second helpings. I thought of what Pete Jacobs said eight months previously, when he won Kona in October 2012, "The weeks before the race I had never eaten as much in my life, and I felt strong on race day.... " *Good enough for Pete Jacobs, good enough for me,* I thought. It was great to see a lot of Ironman athletes there. I was looking through the race programme when something caught my attention ... the professionals' race briefing was going to be in my hotel.... How cool was that? I thought, *Wow, I'd like to see that so I can get an idea of how they think, meet a few of them, and also see what their body shapes are like and how lean and powerful they look.*

I was 85 kilos and thought that while my body shape was good, I would develop more muscle as the years went by if I could stick to the training, and that I would probably get leaner and lose weight, as all the top athletes are leaner than I was at that time.

Feeling great after a nutritious meal, I walked back to the room, and lo and behold, who did I see coming out of the lift but four-time Kona podium finisher, previous Ironman world record holder and the favourite for the race Andreas Raelert. I introduced myself and asked him if he was looking forward to the race. He had a big beaming smile and said he was really looking forward to it. I asked him if he thought he could go under 8 hours, and he said that he hoped so. I told him it was my first Ironman, and he told me to enjoy it. He was such a genuine, nice guy. I didn't want to take up too much of his time. He was with his wife as well, so I wished him luck and said I would see him later.

I went back to the room and then decided to chill out, lie on the bed and have a read of the book that Nick bought me. I opened the cover, and to my surprise, there was a note written inside. Nick is not usually the sensitive type. He is a really nice guy and had coached me with great discipline. He is also a really positive guy, and that definitely helps to have a coach like that, as the Ironman training is so tough. I mean, it's just so hard to discipline yourself. Anyway, the note read:

"Jason,

You have been a great pupil, with a desire, a dream, a vision to do an 'Ironman'. Have a great day in Austria, keep calm and a steady pace. You have to have the skill and the will, but to finish the day, the will must be stronger than the skill.
You've got it ... go do it!

Best wishes

Nick"

Wow, that was inspirational. As I re-read the message, I noticed that the words "calm" and "pace" were underlined. I felt very emotional reading it and almost welled up. It was a combination of so many things. There was my coach giving me some final words of encouragement. The message was a stark realization of what was ahead. Also, in making the decision to train for an Ironman, and during all the training, I felt that I had taken myself to a new level as a person, in not only my fitness but in other aspects of my life. I had pushed myself harder business wise, to be a better partner, to be a better parent and to grow more as a person every day. Here I was also, all on my own in Austria away from my family, missing my children (and enjoying the break), and I was about to undertake the single hardest day that I had ever thought possible. I knew how much the training could hurt but had no idea how much I was going to hurt on race day, although I was convinced I would finish. Now I just wanted to finish safely and all in one piece, get that medal round my neck and live to tell the tale.

So I sat back and did as Nick said; I took my mind off the Ironman that was looming and read 'Swim, Bike, Run: Our Triathlon Story' by Alistair Brownlee, Olympic Champion and Jonathan Brownlee, World Champion. I knew I would pick up some mental tips from two of the best athletes on the planet.

I read the book for a while, organised my room a bit, had a nice warm shower and then skimmed the TV channels. After that, I read the book for a bit longer and then felt tired and got ready to get to sleep. I was still off the caffeine and had been since the 27th of May (apart from the day I did the half Iron), when I started loading creatine and then taking a maintenance every day. Nick had done an 8hr 48 minute Ironman in Austria by using creatine and recommended it, so I was up for that. I did miss the caffeine in training and also loved a coffee, but anything to get a possible advantage. The idea was that I would start caffeine again on race day and then get an extra buzz from the caffeine. Also, it is believed that caffeine can interfere with the effectiveness of creatine, so this was the way Nick recommended to be able to take them both.

Friday 28th of June

In my Google Calendar, it said the following for today:

Total rest; can get some sunshine and swimming on the pier to prepare for heat on race day.

When bike is assembled, take it for a test spin, 20-25 minutes down the side of the lake and back.

I was very aware of not overdoing it as I wanted to be fresh race day, and I had missed three days training the day after my half Iron race, so was even more cautious than I think I would have been otherwise.

I decided to get the bike out of the way. I picked up my bike before breakfast and it was all set up for me. Looked perfect. I had a really nice breakfast of porridge, lots of fruit and yoghurt, etc. … and felt right at home. Almost everyone else there was an Ironman athlete or was with an Ironman athlete. There were people everywhere wearing Asics and different Ironman race T-shirts, and everyone looked really fit, apart from a couple of bigger people, but even some of them were doing the race. It's amazing the buzz that was around. Everyone was eating really healthily and was very calm and reserved.

I went back up to my room to chill, let the breakfast settle and get my bike gear on. I had seen some people out on their time trial bikes the day before and earlier that morning. It was about 9.00am when I was taking my bike into the lift. I had to wait for a few moments. There was someone else in the lift with their wife and their dog.

"Hello Jason," he said. No way, it was Andreas Raelert again … the Ironman superstar.…

"Nice bike," I said

He said, "Thanks." He introduced me to his wife, who was really nice and pretty as well, and I started stroking his dog … that was licking me … yes that's his dog … I said that I liked the dog, and he told me the dog's name as well. As we walked out of the hotel together, I was talking to him about the race and then asked him for some advice just before he went out.…

"Sure," he said.… He looked me smack in the eye and said, "Never give up." He said that it doesn't matter how much training you have done or how fit you are, there will be a time during the race when things are not going well. Never give up. He said that he felt bad in Kona last time around but managed to win second place. I was really appreciative of the advice, and it went deep into my conscious and sub-conscious mind, as I would need that advice a few days later.

I went out onto the road and could see the Ironman banners being put up along the road. I had turned left outside of the hotel and then left again. I rode down to see exactly where the lake entrance was, so I could see where it was for my swim later that day, and then did my spin. I was going a fairly good pace but nowhere near going flat out. I was just getting used to the road and actually went onto a cycle track and back and then back onto the road. I timed myself at a little less than 25 minutes by the time I got back to the hotel.

One down, one to go, I thought, then told myself to chill out. By now I had had enough of the training; I just wanted to get the race over and done with and prove to myself that I could finish it.

I went back to the hotel and chilled out for a bit. I wanted to make sure I was there, ready, at 11.30, as the pro registration was in my hotel. I'd already got to meet Andreas Raelert, and now the rest of the pros were there. They had a separate room for them right next to where I had lunch. No way … most of the pros were staying in my hotel … I thought everyone looked really fit.…

I was the first person to arrive. I decided to sit at the back and take it all in.... I know that is so cheeky ... but remember, when I was eight I not only swore that I would do the Ironman race one day ... I swore to myself that I would win it.... I knew it would be impossible to win my first one, but I had ten years, so to speak, in this sport, right.... So in order to think like the pros, I had to see how the pros were informed, what they looked like and how they interacted.

I looked at all the pros' names in the program and recognised a handful of them. Of course I had only really been watching the Kona World Championships highlights on TV from 1989 or from 2004-2012 and then the 30-minute Summaries on the Ironman TV show, so my knowledge was not that great. I recognised Philip Graves, Hillary Biscay and Andreas Raelert in particular. The briefing was quite informative. It told you about the check-ins, where the penalty boxes were, what each leg of the course was like, the canal swim, bike course gradients, the speed of the course, the laps and direction on the run and where the transitions were.

There were a few laughs when Philip Graves asked a question about the speed of the bike course. It was clear that he was looking forward to racing on the bike again.

As the briefing ended, I went up to Philip Graves and introduced myself. We exchanged pleasantries, and he introduced me to his dad. I told him I was reading the Brownlees' book, and he was quite interested in that, as he grew up racing with them in Yorkshire and is actually mentioned in the book. We wished each other good luck in the race, and then I went off to have some lunch.

Then I saw some guy who looked familiar, but I could not think who he was and forgot about it.

After lunch, I decided to go back to the room to chill out a bit and stay hydrated. I even had a bit of a nap. Then I thought I would go down to the lake with my rucksack and try having a swim. It took a while to walk down there, and I had to pay to get in.... I was really not looking forward to the swim part of the race at all. I just wanted to get it out of the way and then get on the bike, where I figured I would catch a lot of people up. I also thought I would do OK on the run.

I went into the lake and started swimming, leaving my rucksack on the pier. I swam a few hundred metres and was surprised to discover that I could not see anything when my head was underwater. Well, I could see more than when I was at North Fambridge, but hardly anything. Could I draft anyone like this? *Maybe,* I thought … but it was unlikely…. I got back out and thought, *I've only swum about 200 metres; I really should do some more….* So I swam around for another 10 minutes and was glad I did, as I got a better feel for the water and the wetsuit. Still, I did not want to overdo it … and decided I should go out on the boat…. I hired a speedboat and then got to realise the enormity of the task ahead of me. It took me several minutes at full pace to get out and find the lake ... the lake was too narrow for me to take my boat down, but I got a fairly good view of it. This would help me come race morning, as I would be able to site the white house that Nick was talking about on the way out and then see the yellow hotel on the way back in towards the canal. That would be if I had learnt how to swim straight, that is, a fact which I tried to put at the back of my mind and be positive about.

As I handed the boat back, I felt pretty mentally exhausted. This Ironman was a really big ask. It weighed heavier on me at that moment than at any other time during my entire training. It was also pouring down with rain…. There had been none of the hot weather which had been anticipated up until that point. Klagenfurt was notoriously a hot race. The previous year there had been a non-wetsuit swim start, which was almost unthinkable for some people, and not favoured by me. I already knew from the pros' meeting that there was only a 1% chance of a non-wetsuit swim this time around.

Since I had arrived, the weather had been either overcast or raining. There was none of the typically hot weather. It seemed that if Klagenfurt was cloudy, it was considerably cooler. The previous couple of weeks, I had been looking at the weather predictions for race day a couple of times a day. There had been a thunderstorm predicted on race day about half way through the bike course…. *Bloody hell…* I had been thinking … *that's not ideal….* Now, according to the weather websites, the thunderstorm was going to be a couple of days after the race, and it looked like it was going to be raining or cloudy until race day, when it would be boiling hot … ah … that would be a real test…. There's no such thing as an easy Ironman. They are all different but yet all the same distance … 2.4-mile swim … 112-mile bike ride and a 26.2-mile run….

Crikey … back to the hotel for some much needed rest…. Back to the room, time to hydrate and get some rest…. Time to read more of the Brownlee book and take my mind of things…. Get some dinner down me … load up on carbs, protein, fruit and veg, and organise my race kit ... tomorrow is Saturday, the day before the race, and I will have the main race briefing ... swim, bike and run briefly, oh and yes, got to put my bike in transition and relax all day.... Lot to do; considering I have to relax ... best go to sleep....

Saturday

The day before the ultimate test. I had to fit in a 15-minute ride, 15-minute run and 15-minute swim. I decided that I was going to do the bike and run as soon as I woke up before breakfast and get them out of the way early. I woke up around 7.00 and was out by 7.15 and back by 7.45. Just a light spin, bike back in and then easy run. I rode up to the lake and round the transition area to see the part of the run from the swim to the bike transition.
I also had a lot else to do on this day; there was the main race briefing at 9.30 am, then I had to get my bike in transition in the afternoon, before the race.

I decided I was going to ditch the swim. To get to the swim start and back, put the wetsuit on and swim for just 10 minutes would take over an hour. Also, I would see hundreds of athletes for not the only time that day and I felt mentally drained. I just wanted to get on with the big race that I had trained so hard for. My mind was telling me that there was simply too much to do. I could have gone in the hotel gardens and swam there, as that was where the end of the swim section was, but could not be bothered to put the wetsuit on and off, and I had to get up around 4.00am for the biggest physical test of my life starting at 7.00am. In retrospect, I think it was the right decision.

I went down to breakfast, feeling good that I had done my bike and run and knowing I was leaving the pre-day swim. People seemed to be having big breakfasts, so I joined in. My mind was racing. I had brought with me a Dave Scott Triathlon Training book from the 1980s, which I was flicking through. Some of the information, as Dave himself would probably agree, would have been a little dated, but the mental side of it was spot on, and I was mentally exhausted at that point and needed some inspiration as the massive day arrived. There was nobody who could have given me inspiration any more than Dave Scott, the six-time World Champion and probably the most famous person in the history of triathlon.

I'd managed to borrow some nail files from the spa, as I had left my nail clippers at home. I had asked a group of people if I could borrow some nail clippers the day before, and only one guy had some. He said he had a pair, but that they were very personal to him and he did not feel comfortable lending them. So much for the Ironman spirit from that guy; I thought he was a complete muppet. Still, just goes to show you have to be fully prepared, and I guess he was a fellow competitor. Make sure you bring your nail clippers. It could stop you getting blisters or losing a toenail during the marathon. Who knows?

Sorry about harping on about that geezer. Anyway, back to breakfast. I loaded up with carbs, protein, fruit, veg and vitamins. The hotel had fantastic food every day. I told the manager that, and he said that they were really geared up for it, as every weekend they had professional sports people there, often footballers. It was also a top quality hotel on top of that.

So, onto the free internet terminal, before I got into the room to chill out before the race briefing. I looked at the weather forecast. Uh oh.... No storm, which was OK; that was now in a few days' time.... Even though it was cloudy today and seemed likely to rain tomorrow, the forecast said it would be sunny all day and was going to be several degrees hotter.

It said that it would be sunny, 33-38 degrees. That was what I had been expecting whilst training the whole year, but it had not been that hot when I arrived. Oh well ... nothing I can do about that. Back to the room and get some rest....

Then the race briefing ... it was at 9.30am ... and scheduled to last for around an hour.... Nick told me to keep out of the sun, but looking back I was absolutely stupid with what I wore. I put on my shell suit tracksuit bottoms, which were super-hot. I am not sure why I even took them. I had not worn them for a year. Then I put a T-shirt on and a yellow waterproof top in case it poured down with rain, as it looked like it would - but it didn't, in the end.

I was drinking loads of water and stacking up on Dioralyte pre-race, but the temperature today was hotter, and after sitting in a tent in the shade for an hour and a half, I still had the jacket on. I got back to the room feeling even more tired than I had been before.

The briefing itself was pretty cool. I saw a guy outside who had a British Lions top on and got talking to him. It was his first Ironman too. We were both buzzing about the race and a bit nervous about it too. Inside the tent, it was a great atmosphere to have so many like-minded people in the room together. I wonder how many hours the 3,000 people had put in over the last year. What was their story? What were their predicted times?

One of the founders of Ironman Austria came out and started talking about how fast the course was and praising all the volunteers. He also praised all of us and called us the stars of the show. Great marketing, as he said the same to the pros as well, but he was a nice guy and most importantly had set up a really cool race that people loved and came back for year after year. The format was pretty similar to the pros' briefing with the same slides. There was one great moment, when the announcer said:

"Stand up if this is your first Ironman."

Around half the room stood up ... then everyone gave a massive cheer.

"Welcome, Ironman virgins," he said, "but you won't be virgins by midnight tomorrow." That got a big laugh. Then he asked people to stand up who had done an Ironman before and then stay standing if you have done 2, 3, 4, 5, 6, 7, 8, 9, 10. More than 10.... By the time he got to more than 10, most of the room was sat down. He asked everyone to give those people a big cheer. *Blimey, Nick has done over 30,* I thought. *I've been coached well. Now it's up to me to make him, myself, my family, everyone I mentioned my Ironman goal to and the Ironman company and family proud.* Also, I really wanted to inspire all the authors I had published through my publishing company that specialises on publishing people with mental illness. It's called Chipmunkapublishing. See www.chipmunkapublishing.com . I figured that if I could follow through and complete such a big goal, then that could inspire them and they could improve their mental health.

So, briefing over, I headed back to the hotel. First I popped into registration to see if they wanted my six euros that I had not paid the other day, and they were not bothered about it. I wanted to make sure that I was not going to get disqualified and spoke to someone who appeared to be the main manager, who looked me smack in the eye and said I was OK. That was a relief, as it had been playing on my mind. The weather was warm outside now, and I was boiling in my shell suit. I got back to the room and took off my ridiculous outfit, which was really more suitable for a winter's day, and rehydrated, Dioralyted and chilled out with the Brownlees and Dave Scott. Every now and then I would check my race gear, which I had laid out on the opposite bed. I had a double room with two double beds, which turned out to be very handy for organizing my entire race and training gear.

I had a bit of a nap ... got up, had a shower, re hydrated, was the first down to lunch to avoid the queues and stayed out of the razzmatazz of what was going on. Straight after lunch I heard an American athlete talking to his wife about checking the distance of the transitions, so I tagged along, which was quite helpful. I'd checked it out myself before but was not entirely sure. We decided to walk the exit from the swim and then up to the bike start. I did not realise that the start of the run out of the swim up towards the bike start was right outside my room. How cool was that? I was practically sleeping on the course! Talk about convenient. I was thrilled.

It was a fair walk to the bike start. Then he started working out where you started on the bike, and I started to feel exhausted again, so said goodbye and went back inside for my routine of Dioralyte, lying in bed, reading, watching telly and general chilling out.

I had it in my mind that I was going to take some Yerba Mate on race date. They were herbal pills. You could take five in a day. I had taken three on the day of the half Iron and felt strong at the end, so figured I would take five here and that would give me a much needed extra boost. My masseur, Karolina, who I used to go and see about once every three weeks, had introduced me to it and said that it was so strong that once she had several cups of tea of it and was shaking and rushing around like she was on thirty cups of coffee. It didn't turn out to be that important, as with everything else on my mind the next day, I forgot to take it anyway. So much for a plan.

There's so many things going on in your head on race day.... Nick was constantly telling me to keep it simple ... and he said to chill out on the last day, so I became a recluse in my room, only venturing out for lunch. I managed to get in a nap for an hour or so and felt much better. This was good, as I then had to go outside to put my bike in.

I loaded all my transition bags together. There was a bike and run bum bag. I did not bother with the special needs bag, as mentally I did not want to think about it on the course and I also knew there were aid stations every 20km on the bike and every 2km on the run, so there was enough fluid and food going round, it would just be whether I could stomach it or not that would be key.

I had to be at bike transition in my numbered wave.... There was a two hour window in the afternoon. I decided to be one of the first there so I could get it over and done with. I decided not to fill my drinks bottle up until the following morning. I had filled it up the night before in my very first race back in October and ended up with stomach issues and 'the runs' after the race. I was not going to risk that again.

I rode down to the check in, which only took about one minute on my bike. Nice to be so near the start. Saving vital energy. There was a real atmosphere starting to build, with people gathering around. There were hundreds of people around, volunteers and fans as well as athletes. All the banners and fencing was being put up, and loud music was blasting out to give a real Ironman atmosphere. At the bike check in, my helmet was checked and I was asked to sit down whilst a digital photo was taken of my bike. *Ah, so this is how they know it's your bike,* I thought. Then I had to queue up for a time chip. I then worked out where my two bags were. There were separate sections for bike and run bags. Then I set about putting my bike away and covering it in a giant yellow PowerBar bag.

I asked a few people where the bike entrance and bike exit and run entry and run exit were. Then I walked them and felt ready to go. I saw one guy taking photos of the transitions and thought that looked like a good idea. That added another fifteen minutes or so. I also worked out where my bike was in line with the blue plastic toilet cubicles and envisaged coming in from the swim, grabbing my bike bag, taking my wetsuit off, getting my bike kit out and then putting my wetsuit back in my bike bag, as I then ran towards my bike for the big off … then imagined I was dismounting the bike ... putting the bike back in … running towards my run bag … taking my helmet off and swapping shoes, whilst putting my yellow Ironman cap on.

I had a Blueseventy wetsuit, and Orca shorts and top which I would wear under my wet suit. I had my bike shoes in the bag, as I was not comfortable enough to slip them on whilst riding my bike. I figured losing a few seconds was better than falling off in the first couple of minutes of the bike. I had my Ironman visor for running, which left the top of my head bare, so I could keep my body temperature cool and put water on my head when I needed to. I also had a Dioralyte in my run bag.

I had a coat in my bike bag, which I never used the next day, and some ibuprofen, which I did not use either. A classic beginner's mistake: overthinking stuff.

I also had these white arm warmers that Nick said would keep me cool on the bike and stop sunburn on the run. He suggested I could put them on when on the bike, but I thought I would put them on in transition, as with my poor swimming technique I thought I would be pretty tired coming out of the swim, and might lose concentration on the bike. They would lose me a minute, mind, as they were quite a fiddle to get on, but this was a small price to pay, I thought. Then I had the same shades for the bike and the run. I also had a belt with my number in it in the bike bag, which I had to wear on the back when on the bike leg and turn round to the front on the run.

It was getting very hot now. I had taken a big bottle of water mixed with Dioralyte with me, and needed it, as sorting out all the transition took nearly an hour. By the time I got back to the room, I was exhausted.

I managed to get back in the room and figured out my post-race gear. I made sure it was the same as what I walked down in in the morning. I wanted to put my wetsuit on down by the start, because I figured I would be sweating by the time I got it on, as I was quite slow at putting it on. I made sure I had two pairs of goggles, in case one broke (another vital tip from Nick), my cool gold Ironman swim hat and my body glide, so I could get the wetsuit on and off easier and avoid getting a bruise on my neck like at North Fambridge a few weeks before. I still had a little scab from four weeks previously, but it did not hurt anymore.

I went downstairs for my last evening meal before the biggest race of my life and started to eat a lovely meal. A bit of everything. Pasta, bread, salad, fruit, some meat and yoghurt, and I could not believe it … boom … boom.... There was an Ironman party going on … it turned out to be a VIP party....

What an annoyance. I could not believe it … It was really loud and I was at the back of the hotel near it. OK, I was on the second floor, but I knew I was going to be able to hear it … I ate my food and tried not to think about it.... Afterwards, I spoke to the receptionist and asked what time it finished. She thought it would be 10.00pm. I complained to a few people: her, the manager and the people running the party. After fifteen minutes or so, they eventually agreed that it would stop at 9.00pm.

I was planning on going to sleep at 7.00pm. I had earplugs, but this music was really loud. Anyway, I got back to my room and could still hear it … boom … boom ... I could hear the music … I put my earplugs in ... boom... boom. I could hear the music ... although a little less. I tried to visualise the perfect race and even put on a bit of NLP from Richard Bandler to try and cool my head, but I could still hear the party whilst listening to my iPod, so that did not work like it normally did for me. I put my earplugs back in and read a bit more about the Brownlees. Eventually, I managed to go to sleep around 8.30ish, with the music still going on. I woke up about an hour later. It was 9.40ish and blissfully silent. The party had clearly stopped. I sent a few last-minute text messages. Next time I heard back from people, I would be an Ironman. I turned my phone off and then went back to sleep.

Sunday 30th of June! – Ironman Klagenfurt Race Day

I woke up at 4.00am for a 7.00am start. From what I read, a lot of people would get up earlier, maybe 3.30am, to let their food go down a bit more, but I felt this would work. I went downstairs straight away and started to eat some porridge. I had been eating it all year, but race morning I just could not stomach it. I had one small bowl, which was about a third of what I would normally have. Then I looked at my Dave Scott triathlon book, and he said three slices of bread and two bananas. I thought, *OK. I'll have one banana, three slices of bread and a ton of yoghurt.* So that's what I did. I also had a coffee for the first time in a month. I had really missed it during training the last month and was glad to have a cup. I was planning to have three cups, as I would normally have at least that before the race, but stopped at two. My logic was that Nick said to have coffees for sure, but try and leave taking caffeine gels in the race until the last half of the marathon, as the more you take it, the less of an effect it would have. I was still thinking of taking the yerba mate tablets as well ... but forgot once I went back upstairs.

I went back upstairs and had a nice warm shower. The next shower I would have in here, I would be an Ironman.... That was quite relaxing and felt good.... Then I went on a P20 mission. I was putting it everywhere apart from above my forehead, as so many times on holiday I'd put some cream on and it had ended up all in my eyes. I had had some pretty bad sunburn when I was younger, so was meticulous in putting my P20 on. It was already 5.30am.

I then made my sports drinks ... PowerBar Isoactive Isotonic and one bottle of water mixed with four Dioralyte. I chilled out for a bit in the room. I tried to chill out for a bit by sending a few more texts to people, telling them that the next time I texted them I would be an

Ironman. I send texts to my parents, my partner, my masseur, a few friends and Nick.

I felt pretty restless. I was carrying my wetsuit, goggles and Ironman race swimming hat in a bag and wearing the clothes I would wear after the race. There was great anticipation as I went into the transition zone. It was starting to get light. There were athletes walking around everywhere and volunteers and some family members and crowd members hovering around. A lot of athletes already had their wet suits on. I thought I would sweat like that. I put my bike drinks on my bike. I hesitated for several minutes, thinking that I should pump my tyres. I could not see a volunteer available with a pump and did not want to get the mini pump out of my saddle bag, which also contained a spare inner tube and grips to take the tyre off with, in case, God forbid, I was to have a puncture. I decided against pumping the tyres up. I had not had them pumped up since the mechanic had pumped them up on Thursday morning. They felt strong enough. With hindsight this was probably a mistake, as they must have lost a bit of pressure, even though I had hardly ridden the bike over the last few days.

I had another look at the transition entries and exits and felt proud going in. I was wearing a band on my wrist that proved I was an athlete. That allowed me into the transition area as a crowd of people were gathering outside.

Before I knew it, it was 6.00am, and the swim start was fifteen minutes' walk away. I had to change into my wetsuit and put on my body glide and then put my after race gear in the big meeting area. I had put on my heart rate monitor in my room, but quickly turned it off, as my heart rate was way higher than I expected it to be with the nervousness and anticipation of the race. I felt a kind of nausea, which was then replaced by a massive, pumped-up feeling. I decide to take my iPod and listen to some Richard Bandler NLP, which really put me in the right mood. It was the 'Designing Your Destiny' track. Awesome content. I started to feel really happy and confident and was in complete awe of the momentous goal that I was about to fulfil. It was great to see the other athletes. We all had this crazy goal in common, and for around half of us it was for the first time.

I had a Blueseventy Fusion wetsuit and was quite pleased with that. I got to the race tent where we'd had the briefing the day before and started to put on my wetsuit. There were a group of other guys there doing the same. It only took my about five minutes to get it on. I'd watched lots of videos on YouTube on how to put a wetsuit on, and also been shown by Nick. I made sure I put body glide on my ankles and neck and inside the neck and ankles on the set. I also put body glide inside above my wrists, but was careful not to put it on my hands, as that could affect my pull and catch in the water. I asked someone to make sure it was tight enough on my shoulders. When you put a wetsuit on, you should keep pulling it down on the outside and then up from the inside. Keep pulling the outside and you might damage it.

Then I put all my race gear in my bag and put my time chip on. The time chip felt a bit flimsy. I started to walk down to the start. By now it was 6.40am. My time chip fell off. Oh no. I made sure I had changed my Garmin to triathlon mode before. The idea was to press a button, and then each time it would realise when the swim was over, transition one, start of bike, end of bike, transition to, start of run and end of run. I had practiced a few times before, and had my watch off, thinking I could probably manage it. I knew that if it didn't work out, I could restart it and get a time for each leg of the race, which would slow me down a few seconds, but would be helpful.

Oh my God, my time chip came off. I was too near the start of the race to go back and get a new one. I asked all the volunteers and the security. Everyone was advising different things. Then I thought about what Nick would do. I thought, *Let's find the ones with the different hats on, the 400 age groupers.* One of them would know what to do, as they were more experienced Ironmen, if there is such a word. One of them was really helpful. I asked if it was broken, and he went down and had a look and re-fitted it for me perfectly. There was a knack to doing it; he had it and I didn't. Thank God for that. One less thing to worry about.

Pre-race, I had decided to start on the left hand side at the front. Then, at the race meeting, they said they had the weaker swimmers there, even though when we swam the buoys would be on our left hand side. I thought that I would go on the far right, to try and tag along with the better swimmers and definitely avoid the crush in the middle. Prior to the race, I had heard stories of the fight at the start of the swim, broken shoulders, losing goggles, kicks in the face, elbows in the head … it was just natural, because of the huge amount of people swimming together. That's the frantic Ironman swim start for you.

I made sure I had two pairs of goggles, in case I broke a pair.... I went to the front and then had to wait. It was so crowded. Loud music playing. Crowds cheering. Then the gun went off for the pros at 6.45. I heard it but could not see anything. I was at the front on the right hand side. Bit claustrophobic. We were held back about 100 metres from the water, for security. We were there for about five minutes, but it felt like days ... all that nervous tension going away....

Then, finally, they let us through. I was at the front and headed out towards the start. I positioned myself at the front, way out onto the right hand side. We were already split up into three, so there were around 800 athletes in each section, as the 200 or so pros and 400 top age groupers had already started fifteen minutes earlier. Now, I positioned myself at the front. No way, I knew the guy right next to me: the American guy I had walked the transition area with the day before. Then there was another American guy I knew, who I had given directions to when I had been coming back on my bike ride a few days before. I put my goggles on and remembered to spit on them, as Nick advised, so I could see through them. I kept taking them on and off and had another spare pair of goggles on.... Just two minutes to go.... What was I going to do with the other pair? Just chuck them a few seconds before the start. Someone else could swim over them. Then one minute to go.... Put my goggles on ... nice and tight ... 30 seconds.... Look at my Garmin 910, ready to start ... 10 ... 9 ... 8 ... 7 ... 6 ... 5 ... 4 ... 3.... Loads of cheering and countdown on the microphone ... 2 ... oh my God ... what am I doing? Too late ... I've done the training. Let's see what I am really made of ... D-day ... 1... 0

What a release of pressure and nerves ... the stomach-ache and anxiety all disappeared and the rush went on.... The rush went to my head and the nerves to my mouth ... I had to breathe regularly, as I was now swimming the 2.4 miles.

I had thrown my second pair of goggles into the water on the side of me with about five seconds to go and pressed my Garmin with about three seconds to go. It was a run into the water start. Then we were off. I was amazed, not only by how quickly people were running in, but how quickly they started swimming. I ran a few more strides than most people, I saw, as I am taller and thought I would take a few more breathes of fresh air before getting in the water. Then - chaos.

Swimmers everywhere. People bashing into each other all the time. I'd planned to breathe every two breaths and was used to breathing to the right a lot more than the left. A few people on both sides overtook me straight away. I was in the middle of the pier, as I did not want to swim into the wooden part of the pier in front, which I had done during my practice swim a few days earlier. Even though I was on the far right of the three main groups, it did mean that people were over taking me from both sides. I was also bumping into people, as I could not see them when I was underwater. It would stop me in my tracks and I would look up and stop. To my surprise, each time someone bumped into me from the side, I did not really feel anything. That's because the wetsuit made me really buoyant, despite the collisions and nudging, and there was no notable contact to my face.

Five minutes in and there were still a lot of people overtaking me. I must have swum into the feet or side of people around ten times in the first five minutes. Each time I bumped into someone it affected me less, and I just got on with it. I just could not see under the water. As time went by, less people were overtaking me and I was bumping into less people. Fifteen minutes in and I was really starting to enjoy the swim and was quite excited about it. Every now and then I would put in several strokes, breathing every four strokes, but then realised that when I stuck my head up I was not swimming as straight as most other people, so I decided to do the rest of the swim every two strokes.

I had practiced sighting in the pool and watched it on the Total Immersion DVDs, but found it difficult to do with the elements of the race. The open water swirling around, athletes everywhere, being outdoors and the taste of the salt water, and also that I could not see the buoys that well, as they were so far away compared to the end of a 50-metre pool. So every time I found myself going sideways, I would swim breaststroke for half a dozen strokes. This strategy made it easier going around the first buoy as well.

When I got round the first buoy, I was pleased with my time; 1km gone and 23 minutes gone. I knew I would slow down a bit, but was comfortable, and the buoyancy of the wetsuit made me feel confident that I did not have to kick my legs crazily and tire myself out for the bike and run stage ahead.

So I had swum straight enough to go past the first buoy that was on my left hand side. Then it was straight to the second buoy, which was a shorter distance, and then past the third buoy and into the lake, which was only 800 metres long.

The longer the swim went on, the less people were getting in the way and the happier I was feeling. My worst discipline was going better than I expected. Then through 2km at the same pace as the first km, another 23 minutes. So 2km gone and 46 minutes in. Only 1 more km to go and then into the lake.

I had swum the distance before in the pool and it had taken me 1hr 45 minutes, although admittedly I had stopped my watch and ran to the toilet half way through. Theoretically that was more difficult, though, as there was no wetsuit involved.

I did notice when I looked up that there were a lot of people in front of me, and now I was heading backwards to the lake, which was on the side of the start, I was aware that not many people were behind me. Still, this was my weakest discipline, and I had plenty of time and distance to play catch up on the bike and the run.

I was sighting a bit more this time around. Looking for the big yellow restaurant that was adjacent to the canal entrance was almost impossible with my weak sighting technique, so I would do breaststroke once every few minutes to make sure I was in line with the canal entrance. I managed to swim on the side of one or two swimmers for a minute or two, which made it easier until one guy decided to do it to me and kept swimming into me. Eventually he just overtook me, thank God, and just got out of the way. "I'll overtake you on the bike," I said to myself.

Next, the canal entrance and the final part of the swim section. The canal was quite narrow, only about 10 metres wide. Nick had advised me to swim down the middle, as he said it's quite easy to swim into the mud on either side. He also said that it would be muddy by the time I would get there, as all the fast swimmers would have gone through by then and made a real mess. At the canal entrance, there were people everywhere. The marketing surrounding the event says that there are 20,000 fans watching the swim over the canal. I didn't have time to start counting them all, but there were a lot of people cheering us on and it revitalised me and was awesome. What a great feeling. More of that please. I held my position through the canal. It looked like a good move to swim down the middle. I saw a couple of people swim straight into the side and hit their heads on the muddy bank.

I looked at my watch every now and then. 1hr 23 minutes. 1hr 25 minutes. Still felt good. Not too tired. Was conscious of doing small kicks, but not too many, and was keeping a good rhythm with my arms. 1hr 30 minutes … then the crowd was really big. I could see the end of the swim in the garden of the hotel I was staying in. There were volunteers helping people out of the water, and I only had to go round the corner. 1hr 31 minutes … 1hr 32 minutes … 1hr 33 minutes … 1hr 34 minutes….

When I got out of the water, lots of volunteers were helping me out. I panicked a bit, as I did not want to get cramp on the way out, so I said, "Careful," instead of saying, "Thank you". I'd had cramp a couple of times in the pool, where my leg had locked, but did not feel it during this, my A race day. Nick had advised me to eat more bananas and to drink tonic water a few days leading up to any big swimming sessions.

So the swim was over. There was a great atmosphere, running out. There were thousands of people behind the railings or on the bank, watching us come out of the swim and run up to through the side of the hotel, through the hotel car park, across the street and into the transition area around 500 metres away.

As I was running out, some guy asked if I would undo the back of his wetsuit. Sure, as soon as I did that, he saw me faffing around with mine and he assisted me. I jogged up at an easy pace, careful not to overdo it. Looking at my watch, I was really pleased; I had completed the swim leg in 1hr 34 minutes. I was eleven minutes ahead of schedule.

I jogged into transition and felt really good. I got a bit of a shock. It was pretty obvious that most of the bikes had already gone. I knew over half of them would have already gone, but it was a significantly higher percentage than I had envisaged. Never mind…. "More people to overtake on the bike," I told myself, positively. I grabbed my transition bag. Didn't need to go to the loo. When I got to transition, I was buzzing and really excited. "One third of the Ironman complete," I told myself. Well, sort of, and my worse discipline out of the way. The section I most feared was now behind me, and I had swum faster than I thought. Deep down I had hoped I could have gone under 1hr 30 minutes, and Dan Bullock had said 1hr 20 minutes was possible, but none of my times in the pool reflected that, and 11 months earlier, 50 metres of front crawl had me gasping for air and lifting my head up every two strokes.

As I got my wetsuit off quite easily, a volunteer helped make it even easier. *That's cool,* I thought. I looked around. I did not have a towel in my bag and saw other people using towels to dry their feet, so I used my coat, which I had decided not to wear on the bike, as the weather looked good. I then thought about picking up one or two Ironman swim hats for mementos and saw half of someone else's sports drink lying around and decided I deserved it. That went completely against my planned nutrition strategy, as Nick had told me to wait for more caffeine until the last 10-20km of the marathon. Oh well … I lost focus … I was thinking I deserved it, and missed this blue sports drink, as I had not really had it since I'd played football a few years before.

During the transition, I had noticed that my heart rate monitor was not working. This was worrying me quite a lot, but I tried to put it to the back of my mind. I had really relied on it in training. I pressed the wrong button to continue the race mode, so decided I would restart on bike mode when I started the bike leg. I tried turning the watch on and off whilst running towards the bike, and again sat down at transition. Post-race, Nick told me that my heart rate monitor was probably not working, as I had switched it on where everyone else's was on, so it failed to pick up a reading. I could see the time, distance travelled and speed so all was not lost, but it would no doubt affect my pacing during the race.

I remembered what the great Ironman athletes said, especially Dave Scott, who said something like: "Every race, at some point it's not going to go as you'd hope all of the time, but that what Ironman's about. It tests you and makes you discover what you have inside of you. Then you raise your game."

I spent a few minutes putting on my long compression socks and compression long sleeve armbands. This was to keep my body cool and protect myself from sunburn later on in the race. I was already covered in P20 anyway. My tri suit was already on under my wetsuit, and with helmet and shades on, I jogged out of transition. I spent the first minute or two on the bike pedalling and slowly resetting the watch, and had to be careful that I did not fall off. Then I was away. There was a great atmosphere, going out. People everywhere cheering and Ironman signs and the announcer mentioning people going past and offering encouragement. I gave a few massive "woohoos" and took in some energy from the crowd. I figured I was going to need it later on.… I heard the announcer say:

"Point to your number if you want me to read out your name!"

So I did. That gave me even more energy. Garmin 910 in hand, I set about going an even pace. I had everything working except my heart rate monitor. I was not too worried about that for the bike, as my heart rate was always a lot lower on the bike. I was more concerned about knowing my heart rate on the run, so put that to the back of my mind. My immediate concern was to ride safely on the bike and pace myself.

I was pushing one gear off the heaviest gear so I could save my legs a bit, but was pulling on 20 miles an hour easily enough. In my mind, I cut the bike section into 4 x 28-mile sections. I was aiming for a 5hr 30-minute bike split. So I figured that if I could go under 1 hour 22 minutes for each, then that was a 5hr 28-minute bike split. There were 2 x 56-mile laps to negotiate. Klagenfurt is notorious for being a fast bike course. There are two climbs on each lap.

ironman.com describes the course as:

"The two-loop bike course leads athletes through the scenic landscape of Carinthia from Klagenfurt to Villach near Lake Faaker See. The bike course, which has a Tour de France-like atmosphere, contains two steep climbs during each loop, the "Rupertiberg" and the "Riebnig"—the most popular spectator spots on the ride. Cut off 10:15h(05:15pm) Bike 1680 difference in altitude for 180km."

I started off feeling great. Buzzing, in fact. I was armed with two bottles of Ironman drink. I had my favourite PowerBar bottle filled up with lemon PowerBar isotonic (the same drink that would be used in the race) and the one bottle of water mixed with five sachets of Dioralyte. I also had three power bars taped to my frame. Nick had advised me to take a sip every few minutes throughout the ride, whilst staying on the aero bars, and then to chew off a bit of the power bar every 20 minutes or so and put the one I was using inside my shorts. This plan had gone quite well in training. A couple of times I had dropped water bottles whilst drinking, and also came to a standstill and fell off on my first 25 mile time trial race, but felt like I had good control of the bike going into Klagenfurt. About five miles in, I nearly came a cropper. As I was opening the power bar, my bike shot sideways, and someone ended up coming past on the inside of me and rode into the gravel, nearly falling off their bike. A bit of power bar in my hand and nicely tucked under my shorts, I burnt past about ten seconds later and apologised to the guy, who was Irish, and he said, "No worries." I thought it was really cool that when you came up behind people on the bike, you could see not only their first name and number, but also what country they were from.

I was overtaking people quite often. Not as many people as I had thought I would, but quite a few people anyway. By the time I had overtaken around 30 people, I started to mention their names as I went past, if they were from English-speaking countries. If they were American, I would say, "Man, you guys are crazy, inventing the Ironman … I love America…" If they were English, I would say their name and say, "Come on, England." It was a mental game that I was enjoying playing. The weather was nice, not a cloud in sight, and by now it was 9.00-9.30am.

The start of the course really is beautiful, riding along the side of the Worthersee, and the road surfaces were great, much better than riding around South London and Kent. Another bonus for me was that the roads were closed and there were no traffic lights, so I could go quicker and felt safer riding.

I'd overtaken about 40 people by the time I went up the first hill. I saw quite a few people who were quite a long way ahead of me going back down it. Most of them had the cool aero bikes, aero wheels and discs. I did not feel that I had enough control of the bike at that stage and had already forked out quite a lot of cash in my whole Ironman baptism, so decided not to go for a time trial bike and some Zipp wheels.

Seeing the athletes flying down the hill made me more determined to go up the hill. "Come on, Super Jase," I told myself. "Let's do this…." I changed gears a bit too forcefully and, right at the bottom of the hill, thought that my chain had come off. I stopped the bike and then pedalled backwards, and somehow it managed to stay on.

The hill was pretty tough. There were some steep parts in places and then it levelled out for a bit…. I am better on the flat, but was still overtaking people on the hills. One massive guy came past me on the hill. I thought, *No way am I having that.* We overtook each other a couple of times, and I burnt passed him.

This was probably against my race strategy. Nick had said take it easy on the first lap of the bike, but go for it on lap two. I was checking my Garmin every few minutes and hit my first time for the first 28 miles perfectly. There was a really good atmosphere up the second climb. People cheering everywhere. I took a new water bottle at the bottom of the hill. Yuck. What was that? The lemon isotonic drink from the aid station was boiling. Also, the yellow PowerBar bottle came let the drink out at half the speed of the one I was using for my Dioralyte, which I would soon have to chuck away.

The first 20km by the side of Worthersee go really quickly, but then you take in various hills of different gradients and lengths, finishing with Rupiterberg, before descending back into town and beginning the second lap.

I was 56 miles into the bike and bang on my scheduled time of a 5hr 45-minute bike leg. Then things started to go wrong. I got to the aid station and was starting to feel really hot. I thought I would cool down before the next big climb. I went through the aid station and said, "Water." I opened the bottle and threw it all over me. Big mistake. I had just thrown a whole bottle of isotonic over my head, arms and legs. It was so sticky. By now, I had finished my Dioralyte mix on the bike. I did not feel like drinking the isotonic provided. The drink just felt too hot. As I started going up the second climb, I definitely found it more difficult than first time around. Here's where a power meter might have come in handy for the bike leg, to measure my output, as all the pros do, but too late to think about that now. I was also wishing I had invested in some Zipp wheels every now and then, although they were over £1,340, and that was on offer from Nick's friend Andrew, who owned Fudges Cycle Store and who Nick also coached.

Things were still going pretty well. I made it up the first climb. There were less people cheering us on by that time; they were probably already getting ready to watch the pros on the run. The weather was getting really hot. It was over 30 degrees. Later, I would discover it was 35 degrees. The second climb was a lot harder than first time around. My legs were really burnt out. There had been a great atmosphere first time around. Second time around it was a lot quieter. I had been chased by some bees that liked the taste of the isotonic on my legs and had to stop at one aid station and get off my bike to pour two or three bottles of water all over myself. Then I got to the top of the climb and made a massive mistake. As big a mistake as not setting my heart rate monitor correctly. Actually it was an even bigger mistake.

I got to the very top of the climb. I had two water bottles on my bike and picked up a third. I saw a Marshall nearby and saw that I was close to leaving the zone where you are not meant to litter, but there must have been at least 200 bottles of water on the floor which were clearly outside the zone. Changing my mind about pouring the bottle of water over myself, as I thought I would get too cold on the descent and I knew the rest of the course was either downhill or flat, I decided to throw the water bottle on the ground, thinking there was no way the Marshall was going to penalise me.

I then got ready for the fast descent. I felt really cold straight away. I had probably poured way too much water over myself going up the climb and throughout the bike section. Then, a couple of minutes into the bike section, the nightmare scenario. The Marshall pulls over on his motorbike and waves a penalty sign at me.

"You have penalty ... litter...."

I said that there were hundreds of water bottles there.... He repeated the penalty. I asked where the penalty box was.... He said I had to stop, or I would be disqualified ... I asked where it was.... He said 1km. It was a really rapid descent. Not only did I have to concentrate on going down safely and quickly, but also I now had to look out for a penalty box. Every few seconds I slowed up thinking I saw a penalty box, but it turned out to be a café, or people sat outside their houses or outside a pub or restaurant watching the race or just doing whatever they were doing.

After I had clearly gone past 1km, I saw another Marshall a few minutes later ... I waved to him and asked where the penalty box was.... One Marshall said it was 10km ... another said it was 10 miles ... none of them knew where it was.... I was starting to get really tired, and psychologically I was furious and starting to lose it, as I thought that I had actually been disqualified. My whole idealisation of the Ironman brand was starting to fall to pieces. Only a few miles before I had felt like I was one of its biggest advocates and most worthy supporters, now I hated its very existence and felt hard done by.

None of the Marshalls spoke English. Neither did the volunteers. I got to the next aid station and stopped and asked them. None of them had a clue what I was talking about.... This was costing me time and energy, and was also not good for my pacing, as I would slow down and then race off in a temper. I was starting to lose it. Then I found one Marshall who said the penalty box was near the bike finish. His English was pretty poor, but he seemed convinced that it was somewhere else. After half an hour of looking for this penalty box, my predicted time had got worse than I envisaged. I had definitely struggled going up the second climb, but the penalty box was costing me minutes. Then I got to a flat bit just after an aid station and saw some guy from Nirvana Europe, the company who I had got my ticket from and booked my accommodation with.

"Where is the penalty box?" I asked him.

He said, "It's right here."

No way ... he was right ... It was 10 metres away from him.... I got to the penalty box and told them I had a penalty for throwing a water bottle.

"Is that all?" they said.

I asked if I was disqualified, and they said that I wasn't. They wrote down my number, and I asked how long I would have to wait for. They said that I just had to stop and put my foot down. No way. That was it. It did not look like I had been disqualified at all. What a relief.

I got back on the bike with a huge sense of relief.... They do say that there is always a time in an Ironman race when you are tested to what seems to be beyond your limits and then the real you stands up.... The Ironman tests you to see what you are made of.... Well, it had hit me like a ton of bricks. The only thing I had not envisaged during the whole race was getting a penalty on the bike. I was not planning on drafting anyone, as I would be quite far behind on the swim and was good on the bike. The thing I most feared was getting a puncture, even though I had a saddlebag under my seat with a spare inner tube. Nick had shown me how to change a puncture and made me do it, although I knew it would take me ages and that I would be really frustrated if it did happen. Thank God it didn't. The penalty really got to me mentally. I spoke to Nick after the race and told him it cost me half an hour; he said that it probably only cost me a few minutes, but that it seemed like half an hour. God knows how long it cost me. Time wise, quite a bit, mentally it exhausted me and legs wise I had been riding unevenly, so it was not great for the marathon to come.

However, now that I had got to the penalty box and started riding again, I felt a new surge of energy; I was going to burn the rest of the bike. I felt so relieved to still be in the race and felt guilty about all those negative thoughts I had about the Ironman brand. I was thinking that I would still do Ironmans, but not my former beloved Ironman brand races. Now I was converted again and as big a fan as anyone. This was the story of my race, and I had to give as good a go of it as anyone else.

Andreas Raelert had told me that no matter what happens, as something will happen, never give up, so I started calling that mantra in my head … again and again, and it drove me on....

By the time I had got to the penalty box, I was about 85 miles into the 112-mile bike leg. I had been looking for it for around 45 minutes. It felt like I'd been looking for it for days. It was pretty clear by looking at my watch that I was not going to get under 6 hours on my bike leg, but I decided to go as quickly as I could. I managed to ride safely through a sharp turn on a descent that had very nearly made me fall off the first time around. I caught up as many people as I could. During the 45 minutes of chaos, people had come past me on the bike every now and then, as I slowed down looking to talk to Marshalls and looking for the mysterious location of the penalty box. Admittedly, I had been told at the race meetings that there were two penalty boxes on the circuit, so I knew there were not many, and it was my mistake for not remembering where they were.

I'd worked tirelessly the whole eleven months, going from a complete novice to experiencing my first Ironman race, and there was nothing that was going to stop me from completing my mission. I rode like a man possessed for the last 17 miles or so. I was amazed to see one guy draft me and then come on past me when I was having a sip of drink. He had aero wheels on and a time trial bike, even an aero helmet. What really amazed me, though, was the fact that he looked about 75 years of age and he was English. Fair play. His name was Peter. I remember having to push really hard to pass him again. In fact, I was probably pushing too hard, but I was trying to get back the time I had lost faffing around for the mad 45 minutes previously, where I had nearly lost the plot.

The longer the bike leg went on, the lonelier it got for sure, but the extra nasty cocktail that I had not anticipated had really knocked the stuffing out of me.

I had planned to ride the last 10 minutes of the bike in a higher cadence to freshen my legs for the run, but that went all out of the window, as I was chasing my time. As I approached the end of the bike leg, I felt quite euphoric. The crowd was quite small, but people were cheering, and I could hear the man on the microphone giving encouragement to everyone. As I approached the end of the bike, I was 6 hours 11 minutes. There would be a couple more minutes to add to that, as I had started my bike split a couple of minutes after trying to fix my heart rate monitor and resetting the settings on my Garmin 910.

When I came in off the bike I was really excited, as I had just finished part two of the three different disciplines of the race. "Swim completed, bike over, just the run to go ..." I kept telling myself. As I rode in, I was hit by a bit of a thunderbolt. Most of the bikes had already come back and most people had started the run. Prior to the race I had really believed I could get into the top half of the field, which was quite bold for my first Ironman and for being less than a year into any of the disciplines. Still, this is what mentally drove me on in training.

I was also very concerned that I had not been to the toilet so far in the race. About 95 miles onto the bike, I had started to get a bad stomach ache and felt really fatigued … I felt like my body was overheating. I grabbed a bottle of Coca-Cola, which gave me a real rush, and I felt great for the rest of the bike leg. I'd seen Chris McCormack use it in Hawaii one time when he was really struggling. He said it enabled him to finish the race. Up until then he was the world's greatest triathlete in many ways but he kept cracking up in Hawaii. I thought, *If it's good enough for Macca, then it's definitely good enough for me.* However, looking back, the effects of the Coca-Cola were starting to fade and Nick had told me to avoid caffeine apart from at breakfast until the last 10km of the run. I'd already had some caffeine at the end of the swim, when I had grabbed someone else's blue sports drink in celebration of finishing the swim leg without a broken shoulder or broken nose.

Anyway, I got into the transition pleased to finish the bike, but startled to see so many bikes already there. At least two thirds of them had gone, probably even more. I was 10 minutes up on my swim time but over 30 minutes down on my bike time. Then, when I got off the bike, I felt really stiff. My legs were like wood. That did not bother me too much. I thought, *Right, let's try and go to the toilet before changing into my running gear.*

I went into a cubicle, and it absolutely stank. In my half Ironman race only a few weeks before, I had had a wee twice: the first time for about three minutes and the second time for just over a minute. This time, I sat down and tried to do a number two (without wanting to be crude, that's a poo) for a couple of minutes. There was only a tiny bit of diarrhoea and then the world's smallest wee. Something had gone wrong with my nutrition without a doubt. I had no idea what.

I thought to myself that I had the fitness and would try and go again in a bit. I got my running gear on. All I had to do was change my shoes. I put my newish Asics on. I had two pairs of the same Asics and decided to use the ones that I had been using for a couple of months, as they felt better than the new ones and I thought I would be less likely to get blisters in those. My socks were absolutely soaked, but there was no time or no real way of drying them and I wanted to keep on the long compression socks for two reasons. Firstly, the compression may work and I had never run more than 21 miles, and secondly, so that I could minimise the chance of sunburn and overheating. I put on my Ironman visor, which was a real positive anchor for me. I thought, *Well it's not really cheating, as I am doing an Ironman and I will deserve to wear it once I've finished.* I grabbed my one remaining Dioralyte that Nick had advised and then put on my running belt and put it in front of me. I was off.

I got to the start off the marathon and then realised that my legs were not my own. Sounds crazy, and I'd read this before, but it was true. I'd already been exercising for nearly eight hours, so I was already exhausted, even though I was super fit compared to what I had been a year before.

I then saw a guy I recognised from the race briefing. He said that he was aiming for 14 hours and was doing better than he thought; I said I was aiming for 12 and doing worse than I thought. *Don't want to hang around with him,* I thought. *Got to go ahead….* It was really breaking my concentration not knowing my heart rate. I had no idea how to pace it. I just thought, *Let's try 9-minute miles,* even though I knew I would not be able to hold them. Before the race, I had planned a 4hr to 4hr 30 minutes Ironman marathon.

The first mile felt dreadful, and it was only 9 minutes. I felt that I would be able to keep running the whole way, but it was more like a shuffle than a run. I had my Dioralyte at the first aid station, thinking it might settle my stomach and give me a much-needed boost. About two and a half miles in, I nearly went to the toilet in my pants, so I decided to stop off for the loo again. I managed to go more than before, but it was painstakingly slow, and I was clearly having some kind of constipation, for want of a more polite word; that is really the only way to describe it.

Coming out, I felt a bit better. Nick had told me to run the whole way and then walk the aid stations in a kind of frenzied walk, but take on nutrition. This is what I set about doing. The run was really strange. I was overtaking people and people were overtaking me all of the time. Some of them must have been lapping me, as it was a Marathon split into three laps; others must have just been running out of steam.

A few miles in, I found an English guy and just wanted to talk to someone. I felt like I was going a bit mad, as it was such a long day and I was only about four miles into the marathon. My first mile had been 9 minutes, but the next miles were 10 minutes each…. I cannot remember the guy's name, but it was his 4th or 5th Ironman and he was feeling worse than me. This made me feel better. It gave me someone to tell my story to about the penalty. He had done a sub 11-hour Ironman before, but this time around he had missed a whole block of training as he had to have some operation, and he said he just did not have the fitness but he was determined to finish. I gave him my 12-hour target, and after running with him for about an hour, said that it was going to be more like 13 hours.

I'm not sure why I ran with him. I was so relieved to still be in the race and not disqualified. I could not run any faster. I did not want to push myself harder and run faster, as I wanted to enjoy it. No, it was not about time. It was about survival. Each aid station seemed to take longer and longer to get to. There was a good crowd throughout the marathon course, which was great. It urged you on and made you feel important....

I had also read so much about the Ironman family and camaraderie that I think I just wanted to enjoy it. I had been close to tears at times, especially after I had got the penalty on the bike and could not find it. The question of whether I was or was not disqualified went round my head for 45 minutes. By the time I arrived at the penalty box, I was 99% sure that I was not disqualified, as they had just said, "Is that all?"

At times, I had felt like I was going mad on the bike looking for that penalty spot, and the longer the run went on the harder it became. No doubt about that.

During my training months, I had suggested to Nick that I run a marathon or two as a warm up. He said that I shouldn't do that, as it could put me off. This really surprised me at the time, as Nick was an excellent marathon runner. He had run the London marathon 22 times, under 3 hours every time and most of them were way under that ... his best time was 2hrs 25 minutes. So, he had gone into Ironman with a marathon background. When I asked him about the marathon leg of the Ironman, he had called it the death march. I had immediately tried to blank that out of my head, as I motivated myself by filling my head with positive information all the time - probably too much of it and not enough realism at times, although it had got me to this stage.

The weather got hotter and hotter ... I was getting further and further behind my predicted time.... Each aid station, I was taking on more and more nutrition and the Coca-Cola I was taking was having less and less of the effect it had in the previous 2km. The fact the aid stations were every 2km did give me some kind of focus, as it would be to run up to the aid station and then walk through it for what started as 10 seconds, but slowly became 15 seconds and increased each time...

It was great to talk to someone else during the race. It stopped me going mad and made me feel better.... After about an hour running together, the guy said that he had to walk, so I said goodbye and started running on my own.... I carried on for a while on my own ... getting hotter and hotter ... but nearer and nearer to the finish.... The day was getting longer and longer ... but I was going to be an Ironman before the day was up.... I started feeling a bit lonely again, so when I spotted another English guy - I could see the flag on his back and his name - I said hello.

It was some guy from Newcastle. He was a really nice guy. It was his 4th Ironman and he was also feeling worse than I was.... This made me feel better and we decided to run together ... he was telling me about his other Ironman races. He'd done something like one under 12 hours, two 12 hour and one 13 hour Ironman. He also said how he had a triathlon coaching business and organised races in Newcastle, and that it was going really well.

It was great to talk to someone in the same position, with the same goal, feeling the same pain and having the same euphoric reflection on his own life.... It made me feel more alive.... Running on my own made me feel the pain ... I was associating myself with it by looking at my watch and thinking how far I had to go.... I still did this with someone else for company, but it seemed less of a matter of life and death. We ran together for ages ... I could have gone ahead, but was happy not to be on my own. Weird but true. Not something I had imagined would happen.

By now, it was so hot. As we went through the centre of town, I rang the bell of Klagenfurt, which had been lowered. In previous years, you had to jump up to it. I had to bend down to ring it and almost ran into it.

Every now and then, I would high-five people in the crowd. People would say, "Come on, Jason," which was great. I kept urging my new running partner to carry on running when we got to the aid stations; he was walking for a long time....

At one running station, with only a few miles to go, I was just talking to the guy from Newcastle about the other guy I had been running with, who was from Dulwich, when he ran past really quickly and said hello. No way ... he had made a full recovery and was going for it. I urged the guy from Newcastle to run, but he said he had to stop and walk … I said, "OK," and started running again. By now there were only 4 miles to go, and I could feel the finishing line in sight.

Nick had told me to break the run down in my mind to 4 x 10km and then give everything I have in the last 2km, so that is what I was mentally preparing to do.

Only a few miles to go now … I remember the last aid station quite clearly, as it was the first time I saw pizza on it … by now, when I got to aid stations, I was having Coca-Cola, crackers, orange pieces … trying anything, and of course water…. Pouring it over myself, as it was so hot … pouring it on the top of my head was the best. It cooled my whole body down by going on my hair. My visor was only to block the sun on my forehead, and I still had my cycling shades on. It was an absolute miracle that I did not have any pain on my toes. My feet had been drenched during the bike stage and throughout the run, yet my toes felt OK. The rest of my legs were shot to pieces, and I was not experienced enough at running at that stage to understand how moving your arms are so beneficial in running. I also wrongly assumed they would be tired from the swim, so did not use them as much as I should have. I mean, they had not been doing a lot on the bike, had they?

So the last aid station … what a buzz … I had about a mile to go … I decided then and there that I was going to run as fast as I could and finish strong…. No-one was going to overtake me in that last mile, and I was going to overtake as many people as I could…. I ended up overtaking about 20 people in the last mile, and one guy kept trying to overtake me, but I held him off…. Then, in the distance, I could hear the crowd. They'd built a temporary stadium on the street, and there were still quite a few people there, even though Andreas Raelert had finished five hours before.

I knew I was going to finish in just over 13 hours. Not what I had planned, but an achievement nevertheless, and I was still alive. One last turn around the corner and about 300 metres to the finish. I felt absolutely awesome. Although I could not yet see the finish, I had heard the commentator say to people, "You are an Ironman!" People were cheering and waving flags and party gear.

I sprinted as fast as I could and, with about 20 metres to go, tried taking my giant arm bands off, as I knew my girlfriend did not like the look of them, but I could not get them off, as my watch stopped one of them and I wanted to make sure nobody caught me on the line.... Then the last two metres of the race were up a massive slope....

I had finished my first Ironman ... 13hrs and 17 minutes ... "Jason Pegler ... you are an Ironman...." As soon as I got to the finish, a volunteer put a medal on my neck, and I looked at it and felt great. Less than a year before, being an Ironman was the hardest thing I could think of doing, and that's exactly why I wanted to do it. I figured it would make me raise my game in every other aspect of my life, and it turned out that it did.

A few seconds later, the guy who had tried to overtake me half a mile back said, "Well done," and I said the same to him.... I looked at a few other people finishing and saw their joy, or fatigue, or both. I was disappointed with my time, but so pleased I had finished it and proud that I had finished strongly.

I then set about thinking about getting some food in, as I wanted to recover ASAP. I had a drink and an energy bar at the finish, I think, and then went to get my gear from the tent. I was so stiff that it took me about 10 minutes to change my clothes and I needed some assistance. A volunteer saw that I was struggling and then gave me a hand. They also asked me if I wanted some food. There was loads of free food everywhere, and I asked them to get me a giant slice of pizza. I started to eat it but did find it difficult to stomach. It was about half a full-size pizza.

I then thought I would go to the medical tent to see if I was OK. After a couple of minutes they just asked me to leave, saying I was fine and was wasting their time. They said there were people who were really ill who needed help and some people would throw up if they saw me eating pizza. *Fair enough,* I thought. I then thought I would go back to the hotel and text my friends and then have a shower and a massive meal....

I sat down and finished the pizza first, and then ate and drank a bit more, and could feel myself getting stiffer, so I thought the 15 minute walk back would do me good. As I walked back through the park, I could see people still racing. They had several miles to go.... *Feel sorry for that lot,* I thought....

I got back to the hotel and who did I see ... none other than Andreas Raelert.

"How did it go?" he said.

"13 hours," I said. "Not as good as I thought, but I finished...."

"Well done," he said.

"Did you go under 8 hours?" I said. He said he had, and that he had won. "Well done," I said.

I got back to my room, had a shower and some drink, then sent a text to some friends and family and phoned my girlfriend and children....

"You are an Ironman, Daddy," they said. They had watched me on the internet finishing, which was great. They said I looked good. Sonia, my partner, asked if I was going to do another one....

"I don't think so," I said. "It was harder than I thought...."

I went down to dinner. By now, I was starving. It must have been about 9.15pm. It was an hour after my race had finished.... I ate loads. Probably had about three or four meals ... pasta ... salad ... meat ... fish ... rice ... potatoes ... yoghurt ... you name it. I sat next to this guy from Somerset. He had been gunning for a 12-hour time like me, but had nailed a 10hr 49 time. He had a great bike split.... His warm up race had been the 70.3 Wimblewall a few weeks earlier.... We spoke for about an hour ... chatting away ... I said I wanted a break from all the training ... he said he was going to get on the turbo as soon as he got home. I thought *I* was addicted.... *Blimey, that's dedication,* I thought....

That night, I was in a bit of a haze. I was glad to get my recovery food in, and it was great to know there was no training the following day. Then we had to go and get our bikes from transition, as they were only guarded by security until midnight. I walked over with the guy I had met from Somerset, took the bike back into my room and then had another quick shower, sent a few more texts and drifted off to sleep. I slept fairly well that night, but not as long as I thought I would. I woke up starving at around 8.00am.

I turned my phone on and had a really nice text from my dad. He said he had watched me on the internet on the TV screen with my step-mum and their family, and that he was really proud that his son was an Ironman. That was nice to know.

I went downstairs and had about four different types of breakfast and lots of coffee, water and juice. I stayed downstairs and walked over to the expo to get my race photo. It was boiling. I saw a queue of about 400 people lining up to book next year's race and was told that it was the same queue for the race photo, which I had paid £20 for. *No way I am hanging round there,* I thought, and went straight back to the hotel. I went online and had a look at my official time and placing.

I had come 2111 overall. There were 2890 athletes, nearly 400 of who did not finish. I was very disappointed with my overall position. My swim position was 2489, which was worse than I thought. My bike position was 2111 and my run position was exactly the same, 2111.

The next morning after the race, I was relieved it was all over, extremely shattered and did not feel like I wanted to do an Ironman again. It all seemed too much effort to get a time that was not even in the top half of the field and that was 1 hour and 18 minutes slower than I had hoped for. However, there was a voice nagging inside of my head that was telling me, "I know I can go quicker if I do it again … I just need a mental break. Now I have done it once I will know what to expect…."

That night, Sunday night, was the awards banquet and after party. After walking back from the ridiculous queue at around 10.30 am, I spent the rest of the day eating and sitting down in the hotel or lying in my room. I was physically exhausted and mentally even more exhausted. I was eating and drinking loads and did not feel full up. I guess I just needed to get some food in me and to take it easy. Walking down the awards banquet, I noticed a woman in front of me in a pink dress, who was limping. She looked she must have had a really hard race. I thought nothing more of it until later.

They had the 2012 World Champion Pete Jacobs giving the awards out. They interviewed Pete for five minutes. I knew I recognised him. That was the other guy I kept seeing in the hotel who looked familiar. Pete said that he had come to Klagenfurt to check out some of his competition for when he was to defend his Kona title. He was off to the Ironman European Championships in Frankfurt the following week. He was good to listen to, and was "genuinely happy to be useful", as he put it.

It was great to see Andreas Raelert pick up his prize, and good to see the pleasure in the faces of the age group winners and top three in both men's and women's categories. There was a big cheer for the oldest winners, but the biggest cheer of all was for the disabled winner. No way, it was the guy that I had high-fived during the marathon. Seeing him had inspired me to keep going. I started to feel warm towards the whole thing again, but was still embarrassed about my time. Then they had the women's winner go up. Unbelievably, it was the woman that I had seen limping in front of me on the way down to the awards ceremony. I guess that is what it takes out of you if you want to win one of these races, let alone go to Kona and dream the improbable dream.

I hung around for about 45 minutes of the after party. I was so tired that I just wanted to go to sleep, then get ready and go back to see my partner and my two children, Oscar and Anna. So I walked back and was asleep pretty soon afterwards. I slept like a log, and something had shifted in my mind overnight.

Tuesday: Back to England

I woke up late on Tuesday morning, around 9.30. I'd had a full 10 hours sleep at least. I went straight down to breakfast and had my customary three or four breakfasts. I was the last one eating, apart from another couple. It turned out to be none other than Pete Jacobs and his wife. I had my Johnnie and Alistair Brownlee autobiography on me, and I thought, *Who better to sign it than Pete Jacobs?* I asked him to write "You are an Ironman" on it – he added "Congratulations" at the start of the phrase, and I was chuffed. We spoke for a good five minutes, and then I thought I would give them some privacy, as I knew he had a big race only five days later and he was in a different country. I gave him a business card and told him a little bit about Chipmunkapublishing, and how I had been publishing people with mental illness since 2002 to give them a voice, and he said he would get in touch.

"Cool," I said. I asked him for a few tips and a few questions about how he became World Champion, and wished him good luck in Kona later in the year, when he was to try and defend his title.

I went outside and spoke to Sonia, my partner. I told her that I was going to do another Ironman. The day before, I had told her I did not want to do another one. This day, I was totally determined to do another one. Her reply was, "I knew it." Only a few minutes later, I was looking around for races on the Ironman website. I did not really feel like doing Klagenfurt again, as I had already done it and there were so many cool locations that you could go to and several places in Europe that I had not been to.

While I was on the computer, I saw Andreas Raelert going into the lift.

"I am going to do another one," I said. "I want to go faster."

"Excellent," he said. "See you, Jason. In 2013?"

"Not sure," I said. I was thinking, *Come on Andreas, that's a bit soon isn't it … I am exhausted,* but it really inspired me the way that he said it with a big grin on his face and his eyes all lit up like a light bulb. *This addiction is good for me,* I kept thinking. I started to talk to more athletes, and they wanted to do more races as well and improve their times. *Awesome,* I thought.

Jason Pegler

On the way back on the coach, I met the first person apart from me who was really disappointed with their time. He was in his 50s, and had done about 17 Ironman races, I think he said.

He said, "I've entered Copenhagen for six weeks' time."

Wow, I thought. *That's real motivation for you....* I was not thinking of doing that, as I wanted to spend time with my family. I loved Ironman, but doing it was part of my life and family balance ... the Ironman was not meant to take over everything.... It might have been OK for this other guy ... I had no idea what his personal circumstances were ... he was with his wife, who may have been watching or racing with him. For me, it was a no go.

Then at the airport, just before we boarded the plane, everything came into perspective and I felt proud of what I had achieved. I started speaking to other British athletes who had just done Klagenfurt. One guy was the first Brit home in his age group, finishing in just over 9 hours, and he had qualified for the first time to do Hawaii. He was worried, as he could not afford to go. That wasn't an option for me, as I was not yet fast enough or famous enough to get there.

Then I met another guy who had had a worse race than me. He showed me a massive graze on his leg.

"I fell off on the bike and started bleeding," he said.

"No way," I said. "How far was that into the bike?"

"Oh, about 10 miles into it," he said. He said that he had fallen off, started bleeding and got up laughing. Fair play.... He said that his time was rubbish - 15 hours - but he was pleased to have finished his first Ironman.

Then the first Brit home in his age group showed me a photo of his friend with red socks. He told me that his friend cut himself on a rock in the swim.... His friend had said that when he came out there was blood everywhere and medical told him to stop ... he just put his socks on and got on the bike ... by the time the marathon had ended, he had red feet.... Now, here were two people whose races had been more catastrophic than mine, and they had still both finished. It stopped me feeling sorry for myself, and I then vowed to myself that I was going to give it another go. I had worked too hard to just be a 13-hour-17-minute Ironman and a one-time Ironman. I wanted more.... Ah, the addiction kicking in.... I loved the training ... the moments of bliss ... being in the zone ... when you step outside of your mind unwittingly... those moments of the now, when you are at one with yourself ... inner karma ... inner peace.... It was those great moments that could happen in any training session that I enjoyed the most.... Then the build up to race day ... setting a big goal for something....

Taking step by step and following it through until you achieved it. It was great discipline for the rest of my life ... my relationships ... parenting ... business ... friendships, etc. Ironman was here to stay for my life....

Anyway, back to London, and who better to pick me up than my coach, Nick.

We had already spoken on the phone.... I told him I wanted to do another one. He said to maybe do a couple of half Ironmans. I said no, I wanted to do another full one but wasn't sure which one. He said to enter another race, a fun race, and suggested doing an Olympic triathlon at Hyde Park.... It had sold out, so I entered the sprint instead, the same day I flew back from Austria.

It was for September the 14th, Just a couple of months away.

It was great to see Nick. He told me what food to eat for the following two weeks, so I could recover. This included slow-release protein shakes at night, lots of protein, nuts and steak and fish....

I took a week off training and then wanted to get back into it, so kept Nick on as my coach as we discussed the next race. I suggested Lanzarote, he said for a big guy, no way, and that the bike is so windy it's scary.... Florida would suit me, as it's a flat bike and I had power on the flat, but it was expensive and November was quite soon for my family, so it did not suit my life and family balance.... Nice was too hilly for me ... Zurich, maybe ... or Sweden - but they were a bit later on.... We decided on Frankfurt. The bike was pretty flat, and it was the best-supported race in Europe. A few days before I went to Lanzarote on holiday, I booked it, using Nirvana Europe again. Bring it on. Nick had set me some training to do, but now I knew I had set another massive goal for July 2014, I decided to take twelve days off training completely and eat loads of ice cream and spoil myself. There was plenty of time to get back in shape for the next Ironman challenge....

The best thing about the whole experience was realising how pleased my children were to see me, after having not seen me for five or six nights. When I arrived back, they were in the bath.

My partner said, "Look, its Daddy." We had an embrace, and then Oscar said:

"Daddy, I saw you on the telly. Can I see the medal you got me?"

I had promised him he could wear the Ironman medal. Then my little girl, Anna, who was not three until a few months later, said:

"Daddy is an Ironman!" She put her hands in the air, celebrating. Then she told me to watch. She had learnt to blow bubbles underwater and was showing me her swim technique. They start early nowadays. Oscar showed me that he could hold his breath underwater.

Nick was downstairs putting my bike back on the turbo for me.... Oscar and Anna had the biggest smiles I had ever seen and were talking to me both at the same time, so intently and sweetly, telling me what they had been up to. They were both talking over each other, and smiling and being really calm at the same time. I'd been searching to belong to the Ironman family all year by completing the race, and realised how happy I was to be back at home with my own family.

I said goodbye to Nick and agreed to catch up with him soon. He set me a recovery eating plan, which included lots of protein, including chicken, eggs, fish and red meat and a slow-release protein shake to drink every night for two weeks before going to sleep. That night, we put the kids to bed and then I sat down with my partner, having a nice cuddle and chat.

It was now the 2nd of July, and I was going to Lanzarote for twelve nights on the 25th of July.... I took a week off training and then was back doing some light training. Before I went to Lanzarote, I decided to book my next Ironman race.

I was interested in Florida, although I thought November was a bit expensive, and also too soon. It just did not fit in with my family, fitness and life balance. I thought of all the European races and decided on Frankfurt. It would be good, as some of the top pros would be there. Nick knew the course and thought I would do well on it, and he also said it was the best supported race in Europe. It had already sold out, so I booked through Nirvana Europe and selected the main hotel, which the top pros would be staying at. I liked to be around the pros, to see how I could learn and be inspired by them. This time we set a much stiffer target: to go under 10 hours.

With that big target in mind, mentally I really needed a break, so I took fourteen days off training completely; twelve of them were spent in Lanzarote. It was nice to play football with Oscar and help Anna go up and down the slides. It was great to make sandcastles on the beach and not worry about training every day. It was also full-board, and all you can eat was paid for in advance, so there was lots of yummy ice-cream. I knew I had a lot of training to begin on my way back and decided that I would work harder and be better prepared for my next Ironman race. I would be a better athlete and get in touch with some of the pros to find out how they really thought.

This adventure will be included in another book. It includes talking to Ironman legend Dave Scott, learning to swim better with super pro swimmer Harry Wiltshire and doing psychological coaching with Rachel Joyce, which results in me having some much better race results at the end of 2013 and going much quicker in training. It also includes spending the day with 16-time World Champion and darts legend Phil 'The Power' Taylor.

Second time around, it seems more difficult. Whilst I am fitter and a better athlete, mentally it seems harder to train, as although I am still hooked and love the sport, that initial euphoria has gone.

If you want to know about my NLP training, life coaching or consultancy, go to
www.howtobeasuccess.co.uk

If you want to know more about Chipmunkapublishing, go to www.chipmunkapublishing.co.uk and see how I give a voice to people with mental illness. I'd be honoured.

If you want to know about the Chipmunka Foundation, where I raise money to give people with mental illness personal development material, go to
www.chipmunkafoundation.org

By the way i am setting up a Triathlon business to help age groupers and pro's as i love the sport...

The domain is www.141triathlon.com and there is bound to be some free stuff on there so please sign up and join my 141triathlon family.

I hope you have enjoyed my book. I hope your Ironman journey is just as enjoyable. Please do come and find me on Twitter or Facebook and let me know about your Ironman journey. Also, feel free to give me some tips if you have some. Ironman forever. Happy training and happy racing.

THE END

Full Training Break Down

More detailed training breakdown from November 5th 2012 to race day in Ironman Klagenfurt

July-October are mentioned earlier in the books and were selected for a complete novice athlete. They were, more or less:

2 x 1hr swims a week, with pull buoy to teach correct body position.
3 runs a week - 1 easy pace, 1 medium pace, 1 quick pace
2 bike sessions a week - 1 in small ring and 1 in big ring.

November 5th 2012 - Medium Week

5th – Bike 60mins, 17.8 miles. Swim 60mins, 2.5km with pull buoy
6th – Run 50mins, 5.49 miles
7th – Swim 2.5km with pull buoy
8th – Bike 60mins, 20.1 miles at constant speed at 0 gradient
        Run 40mins, 4.49 miles
9th – Goal setting and training plan with Nick
10th – Rest day – most Saturdays are rest days
11th – Bike 40mins at +1 gradient, 12 miles at 18mph, av 215 watts

November 12th - Hard Week
12th – Bike 35mins, massive load +6 gradient
        Swim 50mins, 1.8km drills, sets of 50 metres, 1km breathe left
13th – Run 50mins – 15-min WU (Warm up), 20mins at 7-7.30 min/mile pace, 15-min WD (Warm down)
14th – Gym 60-min core workout, Run 30mins, 5km in 23 minutes
15th – Bike 30mins – High Cadence on +1 gradient 1-5-110 cadence
16th – Swim 2.5km
17th – Rest
18th – Run 60mins, 6 miles

November 19th - Medium Week

19th – Run 30mins, 4 miles
20th – Run 50mins, 5 miles
21st – Run 30mins, 3 miles
22nd – Run 50mins, 5 miles
23rd – Run 30mins, 3 miles
24th – Rest
25th – Bike 90mins – 30 spin - £0 push (+2) – 30 spin

November 26th – Easy Week

26th – Day off
27th – Swim 1hr drafting Nick 3000 metres
28th – Bike 45mins – turbo 4 X 5mins at 260 watts at +1 gradient
29th – Run 50mins – as 15-min WU, 20mins tempo (HR 165), 15-min WD
30th – 50mins – at high cadence +100 revs at) gradient
1st (December) – Rest
2nd December – Run 90mins – LSD (long slow distance) HR 145

December 3rd – Hard Week

3rd – Swim 60mins – (2500 metres) – 50 lengths Time Trial (record your precise time)
4th – Bike 60mins – on gradient 1, keep it in big ring front, put it in 2nd biggest cog on rear, every 1 minute change up one click into higher gear (harder = smaller cog), until highest … then back to easiest at 1 minute intervals. Move up and down through these gears for 50mins, followed by 10mins cool down
        -      Weights 60mins/ Core or stretching
5th – Run 50mins – Hill reps – 10-min WU – run to Dulwich Woodhouse Hill, 5 X reps up and down and 10-min WD back
      - Swim 60mins – Drills and Swim
6th - Stretching/core own design
- Bike 45mins – Turbo – 10-min WU at 90rpm on gradient +1, 10 x reps of gradient
7th – Run 60mins, 20-min WU, 20-min tempo at 7-7.30 min/mile pace, 20-min WD
8th – Rest day – stretching
9th – 120-min run – LSD (long slow distance) Dulwich Park… easy low… HR – 145 bpm or less. Have fun, it's a hard week, so just do what you can, and remember it's just a suggestion - you can chop and change as you feel you need to…

December 10th – Medium Week

10th – Swim 40mins – 2km drills
11th – Bike 60mins – 30 gradient – 30 at gradient +1, 30mins at gradient 0

December 17th - 31st - 2 weeks off

January 7th – Hard Week, 9 hours

7th – Run 2hrs LSD (long slow distance) HR 145-155
8th – Bike 40mins spinning 90-105rpm (increase 1rpm every 2mins) Include WU and WD.
9th – Run 60mins – Dulwich Park 15-min WU – 3 X 2 mile reps, 15-min WD
10th – Bike 60mins spinning 100 rpm) gradient, followed by 3 X 15mins 220 watts (180 Watts in between)
    - Swim 10mins easy then 4 X 400 metre reps and note times
11th – Bike 40mins at 220 watts then run 40mins easy pace
12th – Rest
13th – Run 90mins – 10mins easy HR 15-160 followed by 20mins tempo pace HR 180 (repeat this X3)

January 14th – Easy Week, 6hrs 40mins

14th – Run – Criss Cross session – to park and then upper threshold and back to lower Aerobic for 40mins. 10-min warm down to home.
15th – Swim 60mins -10-min easy warm up, then 3 X 500 metre reps, note times, 10-min warm down
    - Bike 40mins at 220 watts, then run 40mins at easy pace
16th – Run 60mins Dulwich Park (or other) 15-min WU, 4 X 1 mile reps at 10km pace plus 10% (90 sec recovery between), 15-min WD
17th Bike 60mins – WU at 210 watts, at 230 watts, 3mins at 210 watts; continue this for 31 minutes. Warm down to low HR over next 10-15mins easy spinning. This is Called 'Under and Overs'.
18th – Swim 60mins – steady swim 3000-metre time trial (no float), note time and strokes per length. Count your strokes every few lengths and make sure they are not increasing … if they are, lengthen stroke and glide more.
19th – Rest
20th – Run 60mins at 9-minute mile pace

January 21st – Medium Week, 8 hours

21st – Bike 40mins – Revs and Recovery 10mins at 90RPM on 0 gradient, increase 2rpm every 2mins up to 110 and back down, finish with 10mins at 95rpm on -1 gradient – Good Roller Session
- Run 30mins – easy slow/steady aerobic run at HR 45BPM off max
22nd – Bike 60mins – 10-15-min WU, 3mins at 210 watts, 2mins at 230 watts, 3mins at 210 watts; continue this for 33mins. Warm down to low HR over next 10-15mins easy spinning.

- Swim 60mins – Short reps – Normal WU, 15-min drills (one arm L + R), catch up, fingertip drags, balance, 10mins breath R x 100 metres, left and X 100 metres, every 3, every 5, every 6. Main set 20 X 50 metres note times 10-15-second recovery, 400 metres mainly kick WD.

23rd – Run 45mins – MAF test – run at a steady aerobic pace (Exactly 35 BPM off your max) and note how far you travel in the time.

24th – Bike – Spin at over 100rpm for 30mins, 10mins at gradient 0, then 20mins at gradient +1 Short and fast fun session

- Swim 60mins – long reps – 10-15-min WU (drills) as 100 metres each, Chicken wing, fingertips, count strokes, fits (all twice), main set 8 x 200 metres with 30secs rest, 10-min mixed stroke WD.

25th – Bike 40mins (gradient +1) 5mins at 170 watts, 5mins at 180 watts, 5mins 190 watts, 5mins 200 watts, 5mins 210 watts, 5mins 200 watts, 5mins at 190 watts, 5mins at 180 watts.

- Run 40mins – easy slow/steady aerobic run at HR 45BPM off max. This should be at your Ironman pace, easy but not crawling

26th – Rest

27th – Run 100 minutes at 60% effort (35-45 bpm off your max) – the only hard thing about this session is that it is long!!

January 28th – Hard Week, 10 hours

28th – Run 40mins – Easy slow/steady aerobic run at HR 45 bpm off max. This should be at your Ironman pace, easy but not crawling.

29th – Swim 60mins – Short reps – Normal WU – 15-min drills (one arm (L + R), catch up, fingertip drags, balance), 10mins breath R X 100 metres, left X 100 metres, every 3, every 5, every 6. Main set 10 X 100m note times 20-30 second recovery, 400m mainly kick WD

30th – Run 60mins – Hill reps 15-min WU to hill, 8 X 90 second hill efforts (at 15 to 25 bpm off max). 15-min WD to home Dulwich Woodhouse hill 8-10% gradient. More like 20% gradient.

31st – Bike 40mins – spin at over 100rpm for 40mins, 20mins at gradient 0, then 20mins at gradient +1

1st (February) – Bike 60mins (gradient +1), 10mins at 170 watts, 10mins at 180 watts, 10mins at 190 watts, 10mins at 200 watts, 10mins 210 watts, 10mins at 200 watts

2nd – Rest

3rd – Run 120 minutes at 55-60% effort (35-45 bpm off your max) – the only hard thing about this session is that it is long!!

February 4th – Easy Week, 6 hours

4th – Bike 30mins – Revs and Recovery 10mins at 90RPM on +1 gradient, increase, increase 2rpm every 2mins up to 110 and back down, finish with 10mins at 95rpm on -1 gradient – Good Roller Session

5th – Bike 60mins – 10-15-min WU, 2mins at 210 watts, 3 min at 230 watts, 2mins at 210 watts; continue this for 37mins. Warm down to low HR over the next 10-15mins easy spinning.

Swim – 40mins – short reps – Normal WU 15-min drills (one arm (L+R), catch up, fingertip drags, balance, 10mins breath R X 100 metres, left x 100 metres, every 3, every 5, every 6. Main set 10 X 50 metres (very fast almost max), 20-30=second recovery. 400 metres mainly kick.

6th – Run 40mins – 10-min WU to park, 20-min Tempo (10km pace) HR 15-20 bpm below max, 10-min WD to home.

7th – Bike 40mins – Spin at over 100rpm for 40mins, 20mins at gradient 0, then 10mins at gradient +1 and 10mins gradient +2.

Swim drill – long reps – 10-15-min warm up (drills) as 100 metres each, Chicken wing, fingertips, count strokes, fists (all twice), Main set 4 x 200 metres (reducing time each one) with 30 secs rest, 10-min mixed stroke WD.

8th – Bike 40mins (gradient +1) 5 min at 170 watts, 5mins at 180 watts, 5mins at 190 watts, 5mins at 200 watts, 5mins at 210 watts, 5mins at 200 watts, 5mins at 190 watts, 5mins at 180 watts.

9th – Rest

10th – Run 120 minutes at 55-60% effort (35-45bpm off your max) – The only hard thing about this session should be that it's long.

11th February – Medium Week, 8 hours, 30 minutes

11th – Bike – Revs and Recovery 15mins at 90rpm on +1 gradient, increase 2rpm every 2mins up to 110 and back down, finish with 10mins at 95rpm on -1 gradient – Good Roller Session

12th – Brick session – 45-min bike at 200-220 watts (+1 gradient) followed by 45-min run at 35bpm off max HR

Swim 60mins – steady aerobic swim – note total distance

13th – Run 60mins to park easy, then 4 X 1 mile effort at 15-25 bpm off max

14th – Bike 60mins – 10-min WU, 4 X 10mins at 225 watts (grad +1) with 2-min recovery 180 watts, 10-min WD spin at 100rpm (0 grad)

15th – Run 60mins at 30bpm off max HR (this should be your IM pace) – park loop or roads

16th – Rest

17th – Run 105mins at 55-60% effort (35-45 bpm off your max) – the only hard thing about this session should be that it is long!!

18th February - Hard Week, 10 hours

18th – 45-min spin on turbo – cadence start at 90 go up to 110 and back down to 90.

19th – Bike 65mins – 10-15-min WU, 2mins at 210 watts, 3mins at 230 watts, 2mins at 210 watts; continue this for 37 minutes. Warm down to low HR over the next 10-15mins easy spinning.

Swim 60mins – Short reps- Normal WU- 15-min drills (one arm (L+R), catch up, fingertip drags, balance), 10mins breath R x 100 metres, left x 100 metres, every 3, every 5, every 6. Main set 12 x 100 metres note times 20-30-sec recovery. 400 metres pull buoy WD.

20th – Run 60mins– to park easy, then do loop we did on bike (very hilly up and down), 8 times, 1 lap easy 45-50bpm off max, 1 lap hard at 15-25bpm off max, repeat (so hard laps/4 easy laps), then home.

21st – Swim 60mins – long reps – 3 x 1000 metres, (1st as fingertip drill-long gliding), 2nd with float as long pull, 3rd full stroke – counting to keep strokes to minimum and same number per length.

22nd – Box Hill (brick session) Bike 60mins (2 laps tempo pace) followed immediately by 1 lap temp run (80 minutes)

23rd – Rest

24th – Run 130 minutes at 55-60% effort (35-45bpm off your max) – the only hard thing about this session should be that it is long!!!

February 25th – Easy Week, 6 hours

25th – Bike 30mins - Revs and Recovery 10mins at 90RPM on +1 gradient, increase 2rpm every 2mins up to 110 and back down, finish with 10mins at 95rpm on -1 gradient – Good Roller Session.

26th – Run 30mins – easy cruise pace – home, stretch

Swim 45mins – 10-min WU drills, fingers chicken wings, right pull, left pull. 20 X 50 metres going on 1min 15 seconds (i.e. approx. 15 sec recovery) – 10-minute mixed stroke. WD.

27th – Run 30mins – Hill 'strides' – go to easy gradient hill in CP park, run up counting 50 strides on right leg – jog back down. Then back up 50 count left leg… and back, repeat 5 times.

28th – Rest

1st (March) Bike 30mins – Easy spin 100rpm at 190-200 watts

2nd – Race BallBuster 3hrs 45 minutes total

3rd – Rest

March 4th – Medium Week, 8 hours

March 4th – Rest

5th – Bike 60mins – Revs and recovery 15mins at 90rpm on +1 gradient, increase 2rpm every 2mins up to 112 and back down 2rpm every 2mins, finish with 15mins at 95 rpm on 0 gradient

Swim 60mins – Short reps – Normal WU – 15-min drills (one arm (L+R), catch up, fingertip drags, balance), 10mins breath R X 100 metres, left X 100 metres, every 3, every 5, every 6. Main set 13 X 100 metres note times 20-30-second recovery, 400 metres pull buoy WD. (trying for 2mins 05 sec per 100 metres).

6th – Swim 60mins – 10-min drills, 40-minute Easy stroke swim at IM pace, 10mins mixed stroke Back/breast and front crawl WD.

Run 40mins – directly after swim session – 10-min WU – 20mins threshold (25bpm off max) – WD 10mins at 55bpm off max.

7th – Swim 60mins – Long reps 10mins. Nick drills – Fingertips, chicken wing, catch up, fists, main set 8 X 200 metres (note times) WD – 10-minute total immersion drills

8th – Bike 120mins – Easy on turbo – Alternating 10mins at 180 watts followed by 10mins at 200 watts all at fat burning HR 45-55bpm off max.

9th – Rest

10th – Run 60mins at HR 35-45 bpm off max – keep focused on good form and speed, need to do over 7 miles in this time

March 11th – Hard Week, 10 hours

11th – Bike 45mins – revs and recovery 10mins at 90rpm on +1 gradient, increase 2rpm every 2mins up to 110 and back down, finish with 10mins at 95rpm on -1 gradient – Good Roller Session

12th – Bike 60mins – 10-15-min WU, 2mins at 210 watts, 2mins at 230 watts, 2mins at 210 watts; continue this for 34 minutes. Warm down to low HR over the next 10-15mins easy spinning.

Swim 60mins – Short reps – Normal WU – 15-min drills (one arm (L+R), catch up, fingertip drags, balance), 10mins breath R x 100 metres, left X 100 metres, every 3, every 5, every 6. Main set 10 X 100 metres note times 20-30-second recovery. 400 metres mainly kick.

13th – Run 80mins to park easy, then do loop, 8 times, 1 lap easy 45-55bpm off max, 1 lap hard at 20-30bpm off max, repeat (so 4 hard laps/4 easy laps, then home)

14th – Bike 60mins – 10mins at 180 watts, 10mins at 200 watts, 10mins at 220 watts, 10mins at 240 watts, 10mins or as long as possible at 260 watts, WD 10mins at 150 watts

Swim 45mins – 2000-metre time trial with pull buoy - note time.

15th – Run 40mins – Tempo run at IM pace (20-30bpm off max) – get up to HR as soon as possible and hold it steady

16th – Rest

17th – Bike 240 minutes - Hilly road ride to Hever Castle and back through Edenbridge

March 18th - Easy Week, 7.5 hours

18th – Bike 30mins – Revs and Recovery 10mins at 90rpm on +1 gradient, increase 2rpm every 2mins up to 110 and back down, finish with 10mins at 95rpm on -1 gradient.

19th – Bike 65mins – 10-15-min WU, 2mins at 210 watts, 3mins at 230 watts, 2mins at 210watts; continue this for 37mins. Warm down to low HR over next 10-15mins easy spinning.

Swim 60mins – Dan Bullock – Top Swim Coach

Bike 65mins – 10-15-min WU, 2mins at 210 watts, 3mins at 230 watts, 2mins at 210 watts; continue this for 37mins. Warm down to low HR over next 10-15mins easy spinning.

20th – Run 30mins – Hill 'strides' – go to easy gradient hill in CP park, run up counting 50 strides on right leg-jog back down. Then back up 50 count left leg… and back, repeat 5 times.

21st – Swim 60mins – 10-min breathing drills, R,L bi lateral (every 3 breaths), Bi X 5, every stroke. Main set 4 x 400 metres at IM pace plus 5%. WD for 200 metres long fingertip gliding.

22nd – Rest

23rd – Run 20-30mins – easy 3 miles to flush the legs – or 30-min spin bike

24th – Run Race – 180mins – Cranleigh 21 miles.

March 25th – Medium Week, 9 Hours

25th – Bike 30mins – Easy spin session (gradient 0), 10mins at 90rpm, 2mins at 94rpm, 2 x 96, 2 x 98, 2 x 100, 2 x 102, 2 x 104. 8-min warm down at 95rpm.

26th – Swim 60mins – Short reps – Normal WU. 15-min drills (one arm (L+R), stutter stroke, fingertip drags, Fists), 10mins breathe R X 100 metres, left x 100 metres, every 3, every 5, every 6. Main set 15 X 100 metres, note times, 30-sec recovery. (trying for 2mins 00 sec per 100 metres). WD 200 metres pull buoy.

Bike 75mins – 10-15-min WU, 2mins at 220 watts, 4min at 240 watts, 2mins at 220 watts; continue this for 48mins. WD at 160 watts spinning at 95rpm. (HR should go down to 130-140) record what it is averaging for last 2mins tell/text Nick.

27th – 60-min run -10mins WU (HR 150), 4 x 1 mile at 7.30 min/mile pace (HR 180-190), 10-min WD (HR 140).

28th – Bike 74 – 100mins WU, gear changing session, Big ring front (whole session), Start on second easiest gear on rear cassette (second biggest) and hold 220 watts, change down into harder gear, every 2 minutes maintaining 220 watts, until finally in smallest cog on rear. Then come back up a gear every 2mins. Then repeat this.

29th – Run 60mins – Steady at IM pace 165-170 bpm

30th – Rest

31st – Bike 150mins – tempo ride to Edenbridge and pack pushing mostly big ring

April 1st 2013 - Hard Week, 16 hours

1st – Bike 60mins – revs and recovery 12mins at 94rpm on +1 gradient, increase 2rpm every 2mins up to 114 and back down, finish with 12mins at 95rpm on 0 gradient

2nd – Swim 60mins – 400 metres easy warm up then Pyramid 8 x 50 metres, 4 x 100 metres, 2 x 200 metres, 1 x 400 metres, WD 200 metres with pull buoy.

Run 60mins – directly after swim at IM pace 165-170Hr round park loop.

3rd – Bike 120mins – road ride with hill repeats on Whites Lane (Titsley Hill) X4

4th – Swim 60mins – Long reps 5 x 500 metres with pull buoy and fingertip paddles (buy from swim shop), note times, WD 200 metres full stroke easy – long stroke with fingertip drag.

Run 60mins – 20-min WU, to park then 20mins at 175-185HR, WD for 20mins at 140HR.

5th – Swim 45mins/Bike 60mins– Brick session – Swim steady 2000 metres then home for 60mins power session 10mins x 210 watts, 10mins at 220 watts, 10mins at 200 watts, then repeat once more.

6th – Rest

7th – Long bike 435 minutes – Bike ride to Brighton and back with Warren 111.7 miles. Intensity – steady IM pace. To Brighton and back.

April 8th – Easy Week, 6 hours

8th – Bike 30mins – revs and recovery 10mins at 90rpm on +1 gradient, increase 2rpm every 2mins up to 110 and back down, finish with 10mins at 95rpm on -1 gradient – Good Roller Session

9th – Swim 45-min Drills – Jason to follow Dan Bullocks drill sets

Run – 10mins – transition run – straight off turbo round the block

Bike 50mins – Power session – Two intervals massively over geared efforts at lower revs (60) on gradient +2. Start – 10-min WU high cadence 95+ at 200 watts, 10mins in massive Over gear low cadence big gear 60rpm at 240 watts, 10mins easy high cadence 95+ at 200 watts, 10mins massive Over gear low cadence big gear

60rpm at 250 watts, 10-min WD high cadence 95+ at 200 watts 0 gradient.

10th – Run 60mins – IM pace 165-170 HR, with two 10-minute pick-up intervals (Hr 175-185) in the middle with 5mins IM pace in between each. In Crystal Palace Park.

11th – Swim 60mins – Long reps 8 x 200 metres (counting how many strokes with right arm/length going up the pool and how many with left arm coming back) – YOUR GOAL IS LESS THAN 24 – WD 200 metres with pull buoy-note time should be near to 4mins 30 seconds? And less than 5 minutes.

12th – Swim 45mins Dan Bullock Drills

Bike 45mins – Hill repeats – Dulwich college up the toll road to top x 5 repeats (faster each time so easy on first).

13th – Rest

14th – Bike 45mins – Hill repeats – Dulwich college up the toll road to top x 5 repeats (faster each time so easy on first).

April 15th – Medium Week, 10 hours

15th – Bike 60mins – Revs and Recovery 12mins on 94 RPM on +1 gradient, increase 2rpm every 2mins up to 116 and back down, finish with 12mins at 95rpm on 0 gradient.

Run 30mins – IM race training pace at 165-170 HR

16th – Bike 60mins – Power Session – Twenty 30-second intervals massively over geared efforts at lower revs (50-60rpm) on gradient +3. Start – 15mins WU high cadence 95+ at 200 watts gradient 0, Main session 20 x 30 seconds in massive over gear low cadence big ring 50-60rpm at 300 watts (gradient +3), recovery between each effort 20 x 1min easy high cadence 90 at 150-180 watts (gradient +3), 15-min WD high cadence 95+ at 200 watts -1 gradient.

16th – Technical 60 minutes – Fix a puncture class with Nick. – Very important to know how to fix a puncture during a race. You want to be able to fix a puncture if you get one, or all that training and no Ironman medal

17th – Run 60mins – IM pace HR 165-170, with four 5-minute pick-up intervals (HR 175-185) in the middle with 5mins IM pace in between each. In Crystal Palace Park.

18th – Swim 60mins Dan swim drills

18th – Bike 70mins – Threshold intervals 2 x 20mins. WU 15mins bring cadence up to 95 and power up to 200w on gradient +1, 20 minutes at power 260 on gradient +2, 5mins easy at gradient 0 (power 150-180) then repeat 20 minutes at power 260 on gradient +2, WD for 10mins at 95rpm Power 190.

19th – Swim 60mins – long reps 6 x 400 metres with pull buoy and fingertip paddles buy from swim shop, note times, WD 200 metres full stroke easy-long stroke with fingertip drag.

20th – Rest

21st – Run 150mins – Long run easy/medium intensity pace 165-170 Heart Rate (should become difficult only in the last 30mins) can do a few 30-second pick-ups to break up the slower pace then back to the 165-170 HR. Pick it up in the last mile to home.

Week starting April 22nd – Hard Week, 12 hours

22nd – Run 160mins – IM race training pace HR 165-170

22nd – Bike 70mins – Revs and Recovery 10mins at 94RPM on +1 gradient, increase 2rpm every 2mins up to 118 and back down, finish with 10mins at 95rpm on 0 gradient.

23rd – Swim 60mins – Dan drills

23rd – Bike 60mins – Power Session – Twenty 30-second intervals massively over geared efforts at lower revs (50-60rpm) on gradient +3. Start – 15-min WU high cadence 95+ at 200 watts gradient 0, Main session 20 x 30 seconds in massive over gear low cadence big ring 50-60rpm at 310 watts (gradient +3), recovery between each effort 20 x 1min easy high cadence 90 at 150-180 watts (gradient +3), 15-min WD high cadence at 95+ at 200 watts -1 gradient.

24th – Run speed 80mins – to park easy, then do loop we did on bike, 8 times, 1 lap easy 45-55bpm off max, 1 lap hard at 20-30bpm off max, repeat (so 4 hard laps/4 easy laps) then home.

25th – Bike 70mins – Threshold intervals 2 x 20mins. WU 15mins bring cadence up to 95 and power up to 200w on gradient +1, 20 minutes at power 260 on gradient +2, 5mins easy at gradient 0 (power 150-180) then repeat 20 minutes at power 260 on gradient +2, WD for 10mins at 95 rpm Power 190.

25th – Swim 60mins – Dan drills

26th – Swim 60mins – Long reps 6 x 500 metres with pull buoy and fingertip paddles buy from swim shop, note times, WD 200 metres full stroke easy – long stroke with fingertip drag – worked OK until I was stopped and told I could not use paddles in pool because of health and safety.

26th – Run 60mins – IM pace plus 5%

27th – Rest

28th – Bike 60mins – TT Addiscombe 25-mile TT – G25.53 – Race pace level 4 effort (HR 185-190) starting at 170 for first 5mins then increasing. Did not have enough mental strength or power in legs to hit this heart rate.

28th – Run 30mins after TT go for a 30-minute jog at IM pace

Week starting April 29th – Easy Week, 8 hours

29th – Bike 30mins – Revs and Recovery 10mins at 90RPM on +1 gradient, increase 2rpm every 2mins up to 110 finish with 10mins at 95rpm on -1 gradient – Good Roller Session.

30th – Swim 60mins – Dan drills

30th – Bike 50mins – Power session – Twenty 30-second intervals massively over geared efforts at lower revs (50-60rpm) on gradient +3. Start – 10-min WU high cadence 95+ at 200 watts, gradient 0, Main session 20 x 30 seconds in massive over gear low cadence big ring 50-60rpm at 320 watts (gradient +3), recovery between each effort 20 x 1min easy high cadence 90 at 150-180 watts (gradient +3), 10-min WD high cadence 95+ at 200 watts -1 gradient.

1st (May) – Run 60mins – Criss Cross session in Crystal Palace Park loop, 10-min WU to HR 150, then take HR up to 185 then slow down to take HR back to 150… repeat this for 40mins. 10-min WD to take HR down to 130 (see if you can stay running and do this)??

2nd – Swim 60mins – Dan drills

2nd – Bike 70mins – Sweetspot/Threshold intervals 2 x 20mins. WU 15mins bring cadence up to 95 and power up to 200w on gradient +1, 20 minutes at power 260 on gradient +2, 5mins easy at gradient 0 (power 150-180) then repeat 20mins at power 260 on gradient +2, WD for 10mins at 95 rpm Power 190.

3rd – Swim 45mins (aerobic) IM pace HR 150-160 – 2000 metres steady non-stop swim with pull buoy no paddles

4th – Rest

5th – Bike 60mins – TT Wigmore 25-mile TT Q25/8 Race pace level 4 effort (HR 185-190) starting at 170 for first 5mins then increasing.

5th – Run 45mins – after TT go for a 45-minute jog at IM pace.

Week starting May 6th – Medium Week, 10.5 hours

6th – Bike/Run 120mins – Brick session – Bike 30mins – Revs and Recovery 10mins at 95RPM on +1 gradient, increase 5rpm every 5mins up to 110 and then finish with 5mins at 95rpm on -1 gradient/followed by IM pace (HR 160-170) 90-minute run

7th – Swim 60mins Dan drills

7th – Bike 60mins – Power pyramid for muscular force improvements – 10-min WU. Then at gradient +4, every minute do 7-10 pedal stokes taking power to 300watts on right side, next minute 7-10 pedal strokes on left side at 300 watts, repeat 15 times (30mins) gradually increasing to 400watts, 10mins at WD at 180 watts 95rpm.

8th – Run speed 60mins – fast repetitions session – WU to Crystal Palace Park – Run (our bike loop circuit) 1 easy lap (HR 150-160), then 1 Hard lap (HR 180-190) x 3 (6 loops), WD 10mins to home HR 140-150…

9th – Swim 60mins – Dan drills

9th – Bike 70mins – Sweetspot/Threshold intervals 2 x 20mins. WU 15mins bring cadence up to 95 and power up to 200w on gradient +1, 20 minutes at power 260 on gradient +1, 20 minutes at power 260 on gradient +2, 5mins easy at gradient 0 (power 150-180) then repeat 20 minutes at power 260 on gradient +2, WD for 10mins at 95rpm Power 190.

10th – Swim 60mins – pyramid session trying to hold same pace as reps get longer – 8 x 50 metres, 4 x 100 metres, 2 x 200 metres, 1 x 400 metres. Pacing at 1 minute per 50 metres and trying to hold this until 8mins for 400 metres.

11th – Rest

12th – Bike 120mins – TT Watford 50 miles TT – F1/50 – Race level effort 4.

12th – Run – 20mins after TT go for a 20-minute jog at IM pace.

Week starting May 13th – Hard Week, 13 hours:

13th – Bike/Run 120mins – Brick session – Bike 30mins Revs and Recovery 10mins at 95RPM on +1 gradient, increase 5rpm every 5mins up to 110 and then finish with 5mins at 95rpm on -1 gradient/followed by IM pace (HR160-170) 90-minute 'long run'.

14th – Swim – 60mins – Dan drills

14th – Bike 50mins – Power Session – Twenty 30-second intervals massively over geared efforts at lower revs (50-60rpm) on gradient +3. Start – 10-min WU high cadence 95+ at 200 watts gradient 0, Main session 20 x 30 seconds in massive over gear low cadence big ring 50-60rpm at 330 watts (gradient +3), recovery between each effort 20 x 1min easy high cadence 90 at 150-180 watts (gradient +3), 10-min WD high cadence 95+ at 200 watts -1 gradient.

15th – Run speed 80mins – fast repetitions session – WU to Crystal Palace Park – Run (our bike loop circuit) 1 easy lap (HR 150-160), then 1 Hard lap (HR 180-190) x 4 (8 loops), WD to home HR 140-150.

16th – Swim 60mins – Dan drills

16th – Bike 70mins – Sweetspot/Threshold intervals 2 x 20mins. WU 15mins bring cadence up to 95 and power up to 200w on gradient +1, 20mins at power 260 on gradient +2, 5mins easy at gradient 0 (power 150-180) then repeat 20 minutes at power 260 on gradient +2, WD for 10mins at 95rpm. Power 190.

17th – Swim 60mins – 10-min WU, main set 10 x 200 metres – going off every 5 minutes (i.e. swim 4mins with 1 minute recovery) 10mins kicking drills as WD.

18th – Rest

19th – Long bike 240mins at low level 2 HR (140-160max) ROAD RIDE!! – make a nice circular route to Edenbridge, Groombridge, Bough Beech, Ide Hill and home – Did the ride, but not in the same direction, as my navigation skills are not very good and I wanted to concentrate on riding safely.

Week starting May 20th – Easy Week, 7 hours

20th – Bike/Run – Brick session – Bike 30mins Revs and Recovery 10mins at 95RPM on +1 gradient, increase 5rpm every 5mins up to 110 and then finish with 5mins at 95rpm on -1 gradient/followed by IM pace (Hr 160-170) 30-minute run.

21st – Swim 45mins – Dan drills

21st – Bike 60mins – Power Pyramid for muscular force improvements 10mins WU, then at gradient +4, every minute do 7-10 pedal strokes taking power to 300 watts on right side, next minute 7-10 pedal strokes on left side at 300 watts, repeat 15 times (30mins) gradually increasing to 400 watts. 10-min WD at 180 watts 95rpm

22nd – Run speed 45mins – Fast repetitions session WU to Crystal Palace Park – Run (our bike loop circuit) 1 Easy lap (HR 150-160), then 1 hard lap (HR 180-190) x 2 (4 loops), WD 10mins to home HR 140-150...

23rd – Swim 45mins – Dan drills

23rd – Bike 70mins – Sweetspot/Threshold intervals 2 x 20mins. WU 15mins bring cadence up to 95 and power to 200w on gradient +1, 20mins at power 260 on gradient +2, 5mins easy at gradient 0 (power 150-180) then repeat 20 minutes at power 260 on gradient +2, WD for 10mins at 95rpm Power 190.

24th – Rest day.

25th – Rest

26th – Bike 80mins - easy road ride (HR 140-150) 90 minutes spinning in small chain ring on front at all times... not allowed to use big ring on front!!

Week starting 27th May – Medium Week, 12 hours:

27th - Start creatine loading week – Holland and Barrett tub follow instructions – load first week then maintenance dose until race (with juice) – no coffee whilst loading cut out now until race.

27th- Run 120mins – Long run HR 150-170 – easy pace, but hard because its long

28th – Swim 60mins – Dan swim drills

28th – Bike 50mins – Power Session – Twenty 30-second intervals massively over geared efforts at lower revs (50-60rpm) on gradient +3. Start – 10mins high cadence 95+ at 200 watts gradient 0. Main session 20 x 30 seconds in massive over gear low cadence big ring 50-60rpm at 340 watts (gradient +3), recovery between each effort 20 x 1min easy high cadence 90 at 150-180 watts (gradient +3), 10mins WD high cadence 95+ at 200 watts -1 gradient.

29th – Run speed 80mins – fast repetitions session – WU to Crystal Palace Park – Run (our bike loop circuit) 1 easy lap (HR 150-160), then 1 hard lap (HR 180-190) x 4 (8 loops), WD 10mins to home HR 140-150.

30th – Swim 60mins – Dan Drills

31st – Rest

1st (June) – Race prep 30-min session – get all kit together – bike 20mins easy spin in tri gear, off and change shoes, run to end of Hamlet road junction with hill and back, put all kit in bag.

2nd June – Jason's Half Ironman race – Similar intensity (very slightly higher than Ironman pace. Goal – 5 hours).

Week starting June 3rd – Hard Week, 15 hours:

3rd – Swim 60mins – Dan drills

3rd – Bike 60mins – Revs and Recovery 10mins at 90RPM on +1 gradient, increase every 2rpm every 2mins up to 110 and back down, finish with 10mins at 95rpm on -1 gradient – Good Roller Session

4th – Bike 180mins – Long bike/short run (20mins) HR 150-170 – easy pace but hard, 'cos it's long

5th – Run speed 100mins – Mega rep session – Breakthrough workout – WU to Crystal Palace Park – Run (our bike loop circuit) 1 easy lap (HR 150-160), then 1 hard lap (HR 180-190) x 5 (10 loops), WD 10mins to home HR 140-150.

6th – Swim 60mins – Dan drills

7th – Long run 150mins easy pace – HR 150-160 but hard cos its long and you are tired.

8th – Rest

9th – Bike 240-300mins – Long road ride to Ashdown Forest and back plan route beforehand.

Week starting 10th June – Taper Week 1, only 6 hours

10th – Bike 40mins – revs and recovery 10mins at 95 rpm on +1 gradient, increase 5rpm every 5mins up to 115 and finish with 10mins on 95rpm on gradient.

11th – Swim 45mins drills/glide WU, 15 x 50 metre reps going fast, leaving every 90 seconds. 5-min WD with lots of kick with float drills.

12th – 40mins – 10-min WU, 3 laps of CP park loop, half lap fast (up hill to top and down to sharp left turn before fence) – half easy (downhill bit past pond/auditorium).

13th – Swim Long – 100mins – Over distance (Ironman) swim 4km – wear Garmin 910 and note pacing

14th – Rest

15th – Rest

16th – Bike 90 minutes – Tatsfield Loop HR 160-180 spinning small ring with some pushes on hills and big ring intervals of 2-5 minutes – I did Biggin Hill instead, as know that route better.

Week starting 17th June – Taper Week 2 – only 4-4.30 hours

17th – Bike 40mins – Revs and recovery 10mins at 95rpm on +1 gradient, increase 5rpm every 5mins up to 115 and finish with 10mins at 95rpm on) gradient.

18th – Swim 30mins – to pool and 30 lengths every other one fast (above race pace)

18th – Bike 30mins, power intervals 5mins WU – 20 x 30 seconds at 400 watts with 30secs recv at 150 watts, 5-min WD at 95 rev 190 watts.

19th – Run 30mins – 10-min WU, 3 laps of CP park loop, half lap fast (from top of hill along straight round sharp left turn to next right down the hill by lake/pond/auditorium) then slow down round bottom corner and up hill, easy, easy, easy until fast again at a line from the top.

20th – Swim – Long reps – 5-min drills, then main set fast 200-metre reps in under 4mins x 4, then 5mins kick set

21st – Bike 35mins – Sweetspot/Threshold intervals 1 x 20mins. WU 5mins bring cadence up to 95 and power up to 200w on gradient +1, 2 x 10 minutes at power 260 on gradient +2, 5mins easy at gradient 0 (power 150-180) then repeat 20 minutes at power 260 on gradient +2, WD for 5mins at 95rpm Power 190.

22nd – Rest

23rd – Bike 60 minutes – HR 160-180 spinning small ring. All small ring.

Week starting 23rd June – Race Week Taper 3 – only 2 hours

24th – Rest

25th – Run 20-30mins – 10-min WU to run route , 5 x 'pick-ups'/strides… bouncing along… fast controlled, for 200 metres efforts at 8 out of 10 effort level (HR won't have time to respond quick enough). WD 5-10 minutes easy.

25th – Bike 40-45 minutes – on turbo 10-minute warm up, to include 4 x 2-minute hard efforts at 95rpm cadence; Gradient +2; at 300-340 watts, with 2 minutes recovery at 100-150 watts in between efforts, 10-min warm down.

25th – Run 20-30mins – 10-min WU to run route, 5 x 'pick-ups'/strides… bouncing along… fast controlled, for 200 metres efforts at 8 out of 10 effort level (HR won't have time to respond quick enough). WD 5-10 minutes easy.

26th – Swim 20mins – to pool and 20 lengths, every other one fast (above race pace)

27th – Run 30mins – walk/run after your journey will feel dulled by travel-just easy jog or even some walking. Do 3 x 100-metre bursts/strides (with 2mins easy between) to kick start metabolism near the end.

27th – Lots of hydration, take junior aspirin before flight and wear compression socks.

28th – When bike is assembled, take it for a test spin 20-25 minutes down the side of the lake and back

Total rest, can get some sunshine and swimming on the pier to prepare for race day.

29th – 15-min swim, 15-min bike and 10-min jog in race kit

STAY OUT OF SUN AND HYDRATE (with Dioralyte) ALL DAY

30th – Ironman Austria – Race Day!!

July 1st Awards Banquet

Recovery week 1 – nothing

Recovery week 2

July 10th – Run 30mins 3 x 100-metre pick ups

11th – Swim 30mins – Long reps 5-min drills then main set 4 x 200-metre reps in under 5 minutes kick set

12th – Bike 35mins Sweetspot/Threshold

July 25th – Holiday - 12 nights in Lanzarote – planned on running and swimming, but decided to take time off training when I felt burnt out and had all you can eat for 12 nights. Day before I went, I booked first ever sprint race for September as something to look forward to and focus on….

September 14th – Hyde Park Sprint Triathlon Race: Swim 750m, Bike 20km and run 5km.

October 20th – Chilham … round 2….

Jason Pegler

Jason Pegler

Jason Pegler

www.ingramcontent.com/pod-product-compliance
Lightning Source LLC
Chambersburg PA
CBHW022133080426
42734CB00006B/347